Jerome D. Goodman
John A. Sours

JASON ARONSON INC.
Northvale, New Jersey
London

THE MASTER WORK SERIES

First softcover edition 1994

Copyright © 1967 by Basic Books, Inc.

Library of Congress Cataloging-in-Publication Data

ISBN: 1-56821-187-2 (softcover)
Library of Congress Catalog Card Number: 93-74193

Manufactured in the United States of America. Jason Aronson Inc. offers books and cassettes. For information and catalog write to Jason Aronson Inc., 230 Livingston Street, Northvale, New Jersey 07647.

Preface

This book was written with the hope that a relatively barren area in child psychiatry might blossom into a stimulating and productive one. A need felt by every student and practitioner of child psychiatry is a guide in describing and understanding a child's actions and communications as significant sources of information for psychiatric evaluation. The student of childhood behavior and psychopathology observes his teacher during didactic demonstrations of interview technique, oblivious of the relationship between phenomenology and pyschodynamics of behavior. Often the student will wonder how the interviewer learned so much about a child simply by talking and playing with him for a brief time. Frequently the teacher of interview technique can offer little more than clinical maxims and repeated demonstrations of his skill, leaving the student to fend for himself until the latter has achieved some degree of experience and knowledge that approximates that of his mentor.

Although learning by preceptorship and clinical demonstration will remain the core of teaching in child psychiatry, a body of shared experiences and techniques must evolve in the field of child psychiatry. The child mental status examination should not be a literal tactical outline of interview strategy in child psychiatry. The student should use the outline according to his own personality style and in keeping with the specifics of the clinical situation.

Our effort in formulating a child mental status examination represents an attempt to give clinically useful content to the form of the child mental status. We have critically reviewed the pertinent literature and polled a number of child psychiatrists on their attitudes toward the child mental status examination and evaluation in general. Our over-all hope is that we will stimulate these child psychiatrists, both clinicians and investigators, to consider the same issues raised in this study. Our formulation of a child mental status is tentative; it awaits emendation and revision, which will only come from collaborative effort in child psychiatry and its allied professions.

The authors wish to acknowledge their gratitude to their staff colleagues and the career residents in child psychiatry who have assisted in the preparation of this work through thoughtful advice and encouragement. We owe special thanks to Dr. William S. Langford and Dr. H. Donald Dunton, Department of Psychiatry, Division of Child Psychiatry, College of Physicians and Surgeons, Columbia University. To Dr. David M. Levy, Dr. Lawrence C. Kolb, and Dr. Sidney Carter we are grateful for help and suggestions. We wish to thank Dr. A. Bradford Judd, Clinical Director of the Children's Psychiatric Center, Eaton Town, N.J., for his review and suggestions. Acknowledgment is made to the National Institute of Mental Health, whose support to Dr. Sours as a Career Teacher in Child Psychiatry (ITI MH 10066–01) made this collaborative study possible.

J. D. G.
J. A. S.

New York
January 1967

Contents

Contents

THE CHILD MENTAL STATUS EXAMINATION

1.

The history of the child mental status examination in clinical psychiatry

The work of Charles Darwin in evolution and recapitulation theory stimulated interest in the study of children and led to systematic observations of children.[38] The "baby biography" remained a popular device for child study until the first decade of this century. G. Stanley Hall initiated interest in direct questioning of children, which remained popular until 1915.[77] During this time Binet undertook the task of developing methods for intelligence testing.[19] Watson later discouraged interest in the study of children's conscious experiences by insisting on early conditioning techniques.[160] From 1920 to 1930 research activities blossomed into what is now recognized as the field of child psychology. Major emphasis then was on research methodology aimed at the measurement of traits and capacities of the child. With the principal focus on testing procedures, the child was often lost in the process of measurement.[161]

For a number of reasons,[109, 111] the mental status approach to interviewing children was not popular in psychiatry.[47, 59, 77, 83, 84] Although Kraepelin and E. Bleuler renewed interest in psychiatric nosology, diagnosis, and the mental status examination for adults, psychiatrists in clinical contact with children had little confidence in these areas and methods of study.[46, 68, 83, 84, 111] Adolph Meyer wrote in 1895: "If you wish to find peculiar symptoms in a child, you can always produce them by simply arousing the intense desire for mimicry and the suggestibility of the child. Thus you may do the child harm and deceive yourself and others." [111] Meyer strengthened the general concern among psychiatrists that mere questioning of a child was apt to produce useless or erroneous information. In the first edition of his textbook (1935), Kanner outlined a mental status which mainly involved the child's gross behavior, intelligence, and attitudes toward family members, as well as his fears, obsessions, and frustrations.[91] In subsequent editions, Kanner omitted much of this material from his book.

In general, a mental status, based on schemata used in the psychiatric evaluation of adults, was considered inappropriate for children. In this connection, Sullivan wrote: "It has been all too easy to think of the child as a little adult, equipped with the full complement of maturational possibilities that we posit in our chronologically mature selves." [150] The child's language and thought processes were regarded by psychiatrists as too amorphous and elusive for clinical description and not amenable to the techniques of the adult mental status.[151] Furthermore, the mental status approach to the child, it was thought, could not take into account developmental data, as well as age-specific and often transient psychopathology of the child.

Other factors were influential in retarding interest in the child mental status. After the organization by Healy of the first child guidance clinic in 1909, many similar clinics were organized under the impetus of the Commonwealth Foundation.[79] With emphasis on team approach to the child, the social worker assumed the immediate responsibility not only for treatment but also for diagnostic evaluation.[52, 88] A skepticism toward phenomenology and child psychopathology grew. And with the existing developments in child analysis in Vienna and London—and later the United States—the dynamic approach to children was through play technique and therapy.[85] On account of difficulties inherent in any nosology of child disorders, diagnosis was not generally regarded as a necessary process prior to the commencement of therapy. Indeed, diagnosis was thought to evolve from therapy. Developmental findings and deviances were principally expressed in the framework of instinctual drive theory. Perceptual and conceptual ego functions were largely ignored at this time.[64] Neurological examination was undertaken only in the most special clinical situations. Except for Piaget's studies on cognitive function in children,[58, 124] few attempts were made at formulating a methodology for the study of childhood behavior and mental life.[21, 44, 67, 102, 108, 161, 170, 171]

After World War II there was a revival of interest in the mental status for children.[29, 78, 129, 131, 168] Gesell and his associates devised developmental profiles for children. [66, 67] Schemata for a child mental status resembling those formulated by Kanner[91] and Appel and Strecker[4] in the 1930's were proposed.[78] In his 1948 text Shirley recommended a guide for assessing mother-child interaction as well as transactions between psychiatrist and child during the interview and play situation.[139] Both Soddy[145] and Finch[57] described interview techniques with the child patient. And in 1962 Beller proposed a rather detailed model for assessment of personality function in children 2½–6 years of age.[10] Embodying both phenomenology and psychodynamics, his model had depth and flexibility. Furthermore, Beller recognized the wide range and meaning of behavioral deviancy in children. "Such phenomena as primary process thinking, primitive defense mechanisms, narcissistic and egocentric attitudes, weak ego boundaries, etc., occur occasionally in most growing children." [10]

In general, there has been greater acceptance of a mental status in child psychiatry concurrent with the growing interest in direct child observation.[24,136] Thomä has emphasized the value of objective observation of children and cautioned against the subtle inclusion of value judgments and subjective responses in supposedly objective behavioral data.[109,154] No longer is phenomenology universally regarded as antithetical to child analysis. At the Hampstead Clinic, an attempt is being made to develop a "diagnostic profile" for the assessment of normality and abnormality in children.[62] In fact, child analysts generally are keenly attentive to problems of evaluation and diagnosis.[16, 53, 55, 116, 117, 146, 169] In 1965 Anna Freud wrote: "The question whether the latter: namely, direct scrutiny of the surface of the mind, can penetrate into the structure, functioning and content of the personality has been answered at different times in different ways, but, so far as insight into child development is concerned, with increasing positiveness."[63]

Perhaps the change in attitude toward the mental status is related to several ongoing forces in child psychiatry. The creation of child psychiatry as a subspecialty has helped to move the field back to general psychiatry and the university medical center.[96] Research in child psychiatry is rapidly expanding. The need for a more effective approach to diagnosis and nosology is increasingly more apparent.[98] The Group for the Advancement of Psychiatry proposed in 1957 a diagnostic process in child psychiatry,[74] followed nine years later by a proposed classification for psychopathological disorders in childhood.[75] In addition, interest in developmental psychology has encouraged child psychiatrists to rely more on observational data in the interview situation.[89, 110, 114, 115]

Psychiatric methods for evaluating children are seldom given any details in the literature.[17, 18, 109, 140] The art and science of making relevant clinical observations during an interview have been widely discussed from various theoretical standpoints. But only a few child psychiatrists and psychoanalysts have delineated specific technical procedures.[4, 9, 10, 11, 51, 143, 147, 164] Methods of describing childhood behavior are needed.[27, 28] The behavioral style of the child—or his temperament—and its separate qualities of functioning offer new descriptive ways of conceptualizing phenomenology.[33, 155] Behavioral categories that do not depend on established or questionable nosology may distinguish new syndromic constellations with identifiable developmental histories.[89, 132]

In a review Yarrow has emphasized the need for effective techniques in interviewing children.[170] He has asserted that there are few guidelines in regard to methods for the clinical interview, either for research or practice. Although he acknowledged that "cookbook" directions are not applicable to an interview, specific attention can be given to certain behavioral areas. Direction and structure in the interview, he feels, are possible. Countersuggestion and rapport can be used to enhance the quantity and quality of information obtained. He has suggested that both direct and indirect questioning of the child does not preclude or substitute for doll-play and other projective interview techniques. Thus there are many possible approaches to the interview of the child, each playing in concert with the others.

Werkman has attempted a formulation of the "technical aspects of the conduct of the diagnostic or therapeutic interview." [164] He regards play as basic to the diagnostic interview. The child's manipulation of symbolic objects, he believes, is one of best means of obtaining from the child affective and cognitive material. Werkman has provided useful guidelines for handling play activities during the interview. He has also discussed various methods of questioning a child. He agrees with Simmons that "the information to be obtained from the psychiatric examination is the same as that needed for the mental status in examining adults; i.e., orientation, mode of thought, fantasies, ambitions, self-concept, interpersonal relationships, etc." Methods of obtaining such clinical data, however, are not explicit in these reports. This omission is common to most discussions of the mental status examination of children.[109]

Deutsch and Murphy have stressed the need for systematizing an approach to the clinical interview.[46] They have cautioned that the "interviewer must not be at the mercy of the patient's intentions and inclinations to give information. . . . On the contrary, knowledge of the personality traits in different diseases tells the interviewer how and where to guide the patient's thoughts." [46] Kahn and Cannell have viewed Deutsch and Murphy's approach as role-playing. "Children will respond to systems, be they directive or non-directive; the clinician, however, may be so caught up in the self-imposed strait jacket of technique, that he will fail to respond to the children's communications." [90] A child psychiatrist must be non-directive part of the time, especially within the "free-play" part of the examination. But even if the child spontaneously describes the play activity, it is often necessary to intervene, preferably with leading declarative statements rather than direct questions, in order to get an elaboration of the child's thoughts and fantasies.

In reviewing the literature, it is apparent that there are few comprehensive discussions of the contents of the psychiatric examination in children.[73] Those that do exist are heavy in form and light in content. Many psychiatrists have written about specific aspects of the clinical evaluation.[21] Some have confused the mental status and evaluation in general with treatment.[2, 35, 106, 168] Other child psychiatrists have given overevaluation to clinical psychology and social work. Still others have stressed the necessity of including the family in the evaluation of the child.[108, 158] An already nebulous diagnostic process is now extended to the child's family. Methods for evaluating the child in conjoint sessions with parents must be further developed.[1, 108] And along with the same traditional behavioral items of the mental status, neurological and developmental assessments must be built into the child mental status.[123, 124] Piagetian interview methods and measures of cognitive development should be added, to some degree, to the assessment of both normality and abnormality in childhood.[99]

The clinical, community mental health and research needs for more effective methods of clinical assessment in child psychiatry are enormous. Likewise, the possibilities for developing effective and comprehensive clinical and research evaluative techniques are great.

2.

A survey of the mental status examination in child psychiatry: prevailing models and attitudes

There are few reviews of the technical aspects of the diagnostic interview in child psychiatry.[109] Nevertheless, a wide diversity of opinion exists as far as principles and form of the interview are concerned. Little agreement as to what is required for the assessment of a child mental status is found in the literature. Furthermore, no statement of the predictive or planning value of a child mental status is made.

Discussions of the child mental status underscore the nuclear role of play therapy in diagnosis. Play is often regarded as the only diagnostic technique in child psychiatry—the only medium through which the child's fantasies can be extracted and understood. The "conversational" approach to the interview is in general discouraged. Passive play is usually viewed as the procedure of choice for diagnosis and therapy; and if a child must be asked a question, the interrogative approach should be indirect, or the question should be tempered with a generalization.

Because of the lack of agreement in the literature as to

what constitutes a child mental status, we decided to conduct a survey of child psychiatrists for the purpose of determining prevailing attitudes and practices toward the mental status examination of the child. Fifty-six letters were sent to university divisional and departmental chiefs, clinic directors, and clinical investigators in child psychiatry, as well as directors of child guidance clinics. The names of those polled were selected on the basis of child psychiatric facilities accredited by the American Board of Psychiatry and Neurology. Thirty-seven questionnaires were sent to child psychiatrists in the United States. Nineteen were mailed to child psychiatrists working in medical centers of Great Britain, France, Germany, and the Scandinavian countries.

The results of the survey are indicated in Table 1. The tabulations demonstrate that approximately one-half of American and European child psychiatrists were using various types of mental status outlines in 1965. General comments about the clinical value of the mental status for children and enclosures outlining the mental status currently used by the respondent were especially informative. A number of American child psychiatrists felt that a mental status guide would be helpful if it could be devised. Several indicated that they themselves intended to formulate such a guide in the future. Some asserted that there is a pressing need for a child mental status. There was, in general, agreement that the child mental status, as it currently exists, is primitive and crude in comparison with the adult form. But those who believed that the child mental status could be made clinically effective doubted its value for teaching. In this connection, only three American respondents mentioned using GAP Report #38: "The Diagnostic Process in Child Psychiatry." [74] They insisted that their residents in child psychiatry be familiar with this report, but they relied on demonstrations and seminars for the teaching of specific techniques for assessment of the psychological, emotional, and developmental status of the child.

Table 1: RESULTS OF SURVEY: USE OF CHILD MENTAL STATUS
IN AMERICAN AND EUROPEAN CHILD PSYCHIATRY
FACILITIES

	American (N = 37)	*European* (N = 17)
Using Mental Status	10	5
Not Using Mental Status	20	10
No Reply	7	2

In two instances replies reflected the attitude that a mental status examination for the child is as meaningful, feasible, and as diagnostically significant as that for the adult. One psychiatrist surveyed stated that he found it dangerous to rely on the social history and psychological tests alone in the assessment of a child. In addition, he thought that play therapy was "too time-consuming" for a diagnostic evaluation. Play activities, he asserted, have to be supplemented by direct questioning, the nature of which depended upon the age of the child and the intent of the play. Over a dozen child psychiatrists supplied history forms. They doubted, however, that a mental status examination was useful for children younger than adolescents.

Nevertheless, even those respondents who doubted the everyday clinical value of a child mental status examination indicated that for follow-up and longitudinal studies a mental status classification of behavior is invaluable. Four psychiatrists suggested rating scales and behavioral schedules in lieu of a mental status approach. They believed that these techniques were more accurate and efficient than a mental status in detailing psychopathology. Three psychiatrists stressed the need for a mental status combining neurological, neuropsychological, and psychiatric parameters. A few respondents despaired at the prospects of formalizing a mental status for children. They also doubted whether a formalized approach could be successfully taught to residents. One psychiatrist insisted on the need to differentiate between phenomenology and dynamics, as well as etiology, in doing the mental status of a child: "One should describe the child's behavior—not the examiner's inferences about the behavior."

Several child psychiatrists discussed their attempts to amend and modify the adult mental status examination for individual youngsters. They believed that their mental status was valuable only to the medical student. Several respondents stated that mental status information could be obtained only through interviews with parents who should be encouraged to talk about the child's problems, school behavior, general development, and family history. They placed little credence in the value of direct observation of the child. Another psychiatrist remarked that the mental status is important only for inpatients who must be regularly followed. Another view held that a formalized approach to the interview has merit only if a report to an outside agency is indicated; if so, the format should be along traditional mental status lines, including "orientation, memory, judgment and flow of speech."

Only three child psychiatrists indicated that they believed preschool and early latency children could carry on meaningfully problem-oriented discussion. For them, play activities are useful only in those instances in which the youngster is blocked in speech. Many respondents asserted that the traditional adult mental status is highly inappropriate to the needs of the child and can only result in mobilizing a child's hostility and anxiety. Another frequent statement was that the mental and the developmental status provide two separate kinds of information which cannot be combined for clinical purposes. In addition, a mental status scheme serves only the purpose of communicating to professional personnel outside of the institution where the examination is done. Another opinion was that a detailed narrative account of a contact with the child is the best way of developing an objective yet dynamic picture of the child. It was stressed, however, that the child's physical appearance, movements, and speech should be recorded, and dynamic and etiological interpretations of behavior be separately made.

Those respondents who mentioned that questioning the child during the interview can be meaningfully done were quick to add that questions should be buffered with generalizations. Furthermore, sexual material should not routinely be introduced into the initial examination. They used fantasy material, such as human figure drawings, "three wishes," Despert's fables, favorite heroes, recurrent dreams, narratives of favorite television characters or movie scenes, preferred animals, and happiest and saddest memories. With careful questioning of the child about his comments projected in fantasy material, the child, they believed, could be led to more affect-laden components of conflict. The opinion was expressed that no distinction should be made between the psychological test battery and the psychiatric examination. Not a few respondents stressed that the approach to the child should be "psychological and not medical." There was no point, they thought, in doing physical and neurological testing.

It was often said that a mental status examination is too static—that the preferred approach to an interview with a child is to blend developmental and psychiatric information, extracted from verbal, projective, and historical material obtained during the intake evaluation of the child. Several child psychiatrists stated that the mental status approach is more applicable to adult patients and that psychological testing corresponds most closely to the adult mental status.

At three American medical centers, Anna Freud's outline for the assessment of childhood disturbances is employed.[62] This outline is preferred by them because a comprehensive metapsychological picture of the child, they believe, is most essential in the evaluation of a child. Several child analysts mentioned that only through therapy is an assessment of the child possible. Three therapists asserted that the interaction of the patient with his family is the key to understanding the child's behavior. They suggested giving several motivational interpretations to the family after the child's initial interview in order to assess the parents' responsiveness to the therapist. They left the collection of traditional historical and developmental information to the psychiatric social worker. One respondent stated that he had no formalized approach to the child. "It is a matter of relationship; one must maintain a neutral contact." Several people felt that the most significant observable behavior was phenomena which indicated transient regressions.

Only a few psychiatrists elaborated their evaluative approach to children. Several believed that a medical and developmental history should be elicited; but that, apart from this, the interview should be allowed to take its own course. Any approach to interviewing children, it was stated, must suit the temperament of the psychiatrist. Several individuals asserted that a mental status review might come at the conclusion of the diagnostic interview. In their review, they would include the parents' statement of the problem as well as the child's behavior —thinking, affect, insight and judgment, combined with calculations, memory, and ability in handling similarities-differences. Another proposal held that the assessment of behavior should be based primarily on the mode through which the child separated from his mother. The remainder of the interview should consist of play activities, reading and writing, and a brief neurological examination. Four psychiatrists attached copies of their own mental status examination for children. The mental status outlines stressed appearance and behavior, under which was listed posture, motor activity, speech, thought, and affect.

European child psychiatrists tended to be more phenomenological in their evalution of children than their American counterparts. In addition, they stressed neurophysiological development and often included a neurological appraisal of the child in the body of the mental status: gait, gross and fine movements and coordination, hearing, vision, stereognosis, laterality, body image and tongue and soft palate movements.

Psychological tests were regarded by two respondents as the most effective means for the evaluation of the preschool child. They did not consider direct observation—either by the psychiatrist or by the nursery school teacher —as revealing as testing. One psychiatrist equated psychological testing with the mental status for all ages. The most commonly mentioned tests were the Children's

Apperceptive Test (CAT), the Thematic Apperception Test (TAT), the Rorschach Psychodiagnostic Battery, the Mackover Sentence Completion Test, and the Howells-Lickorish Family Relations Indicator.

Survey of the models of, and attitudes toward, the child mental status demonstrated not only an enthusiastic interest in the topic but also considerable doubt, confusion, and bias in the theory and practice of the child mental status and in the diagnostic process itself. There is a predominant feeling among psychiatrists that the psychiatric evaluation of the child is a personal matter, depending on the psychiatrist's experience and virtuosity; it defies description and communication. Nevertheless, the replies demonstrate a growing world-wide interest in the many fundamental problems of child psychiatry. A flexible and objective international nosology, diagnostic method, and international classificatory system are needed.[172]

3.

The theory and practice
of the child
mental status examination

The mental status examination of children is one part of the three-dimensional diagnostic process. The first dimension emerges from the study of a child's family and social milieu as well as from the historical evolution of the presenting problem. In child psychiatry, this information is derived from reports gathered from parents, schools, and other referral sources. Tentative inferences are made about possible pathogenic factors operating in the child's present as well as past environment. Parents are the mainstay of historical information about the child. They are not only reporters of the child's psychopathology; they are participants.[108] As Caplan indicates: "The artificial isolation of pathology in the child from the pathogenic factors in the environment, which is possible in older patients, is here more obviously inadvisable." [30]

The second dimension is the developmental biological profile, a synthesis of information from the parents' report of the child's physical growth and adaptive development and the family physician's examination report, as well as results of previous neurological and psychiatric examinations. The second dimension thus represents a continuum of descriptive developmental information up to and including the present. Again the parents are cast in the role of the principal informants. They are, of course, closer to the child than teachers, physicians, or other professional people. They are best equipped as far as experience with their child is concerned, but least capable in reporting objective impressions of the child. Social histories gathered from parents are of great importance in understanding the composite child-rearing attitudes and ongoing practices of mental hygiene in the home. The well-prepared compiler of social history, whether social worker, psychologist, or psychiatrist, evaluates the parents in a dynamic framework while gathering diagnostic information about the child.

Unfortunately, parental reports are not very valid. As Wenar notes, social and developmental histories provide a great deal of information in proportion to the investment of professional time, but the information is often unreliable.[163] These histories are particularly unreliable on many facets of child development which often unduly influence the results of child psychodiagnostics. The unreliable areas in the developmental history include child-rearing practices such as weaning, toilet training, childhood illnesses, and estimates of interpersonal relationships in the home. Nevertheless, the parental report, even if unreliable, presents the most comprehensive view of the child in longitudinal profile. Despite the great limitations in reliability of the parental report, no child diagnostic evaluation can proceed in its absence. The psychiatrist must familiarize himself with its contents during the study of a child. The prior knowledge of symptoms, developmental deviations, or limitations of the child facilitates the diagnostic interview and provides information about some areas of behavior which the child is disinclined or ill-prepared to communicate.[166] The parents' report of the child may be consonant with the child's observed behavior and self-description. Marked incongruity is always diagnostically significant, particularly if the child has been over- or underestimated in the parents' report.

The third dimension is based on the phenomenological evaluation of the child. It comprises a psychiatric and, if indicated, a neurological examination of the child, along with the results of psychological testing. It is in the psychiatric examination that the mental state of the child is assessed.

The mental status examination of children occupies a critical position in the diagnostic procedure, because it provides the cornerstone for the synthesis of developmental, transactional, and psychodynamic data and gives structure and function to formulation, disposition, treatment, and prognosis of the child. An incomplete, perfunctory mental status examination of children can result in an inaccurate or incomplete final psychodiagnostic formulation, top-heavy with theory and weakly based on developmental and clinical data. Furthermore, a mental status of the child, as presented in the initial interview, provides a baseline for clinical follow-up studies in later years. If treatment is necessary for the child, the mental status will remind the therapist of the initial picture of the child's functioning. If the child is later followed or reevaluated by another child psychiatrist, it can emphasize to the second psychiatrist deviations, arrest, or regression in development during the interim. The child's initial mental status provides an outline for future comparison needed for research in the natural history of child psychopathology and the effectiveness of various therapies. The efficacy of information—retrieval systems, "case banks" for follow-up studies, and other computerized clinical data programs—depends on the adequacy of clinical data collected in diagnostic evaluations.

The mental status examination in general psychiatry is a descriptive document which portrays a patient's appearance, perception, affects, cognition, and general intellectual development. In adult psychiatry it has become associated with a search for defects in orientation, memory, cognition, perception, speech, and affect. The very presence or absence of symptom-clusters or responses in the examination is given semiotic and etiologic meaning. The mental state and developmental profile of the child, however, cannot be similarly assessed. The child psychiatrist is confronted with a sampling difficulty, which is not the same as that of the examination of the adult. The "off day" or "off moment" of a child, although significant in itself, is reflected in the child's thinking and behavior to an extent far greater than is the rule with adults. The adult's coping devices in the interview provide descriptive and dynamic data of a qualitative nature. On the other hand, a child's coping style in an interview is immediately related to developmental attainment and ego equipment. Adult behavior is only partially verbalized, partly evident in gestures and facial expressions, and at times largely distorted and disguised. The child's responses, however, are more immediate, direct, and are transformed into activity and play. Rarely does the child actively reflect on his remarks to the psychiatrist. Children are curious; they can wonder aloud, but their reflections usually involve persons and objects of little immediate concern.

Whether thought disorders exist in young children remains a controversial issue. Important also is the question of definition of thought disorder in children. Is it overinclusive thinking, an inability to inhibit external sensation and thoughts?[172] Some child psychiatrists believe that formal thought disorders in children are mainly related to toxic phenomena and reflect disruptive physical insults to the integrity of the CNS. Others view thought disorders in children as benign instances of transient regressive states. Still other child psychiatrists point to dereistic thinking as pathognomonic of autistic children, indicative of severe ego deviation and impairment in object relations.

It does not seem sufficient in a mental status to indicate whether thought disorder is merely present or not. A quantitative statement of the frequency of thought disorder is essential. The relative severity of primary process thinking should be determined by its preponderance in the verbal productions of the child. If the child speaks in a predominantly primary process mode with gross displacements, distortions, generalizations, and repetitiveness paramount, the pervasiveness of this kind of thinking and specific examples should be noted and recorded in the mental status. Occasional evidence of this mode of thinking, however, does not necessarily indicate psychosis. The degree of primary process thinking in children is assessed in the mental status examination by first noting the child's spontaneous cognitive productions and secondly by observing his general behavioral responses, most critically those related to the psychiatrist.

Eisenberg has remarked on the relative infrequency of hallucination in children which "is difficult to reconcile with a literal theory of regression to primitive modes of thought; being closer to this infantile era and having a less well developed ego structure, the child might be expected to 'regress' more readily, but he does not." [49] Children, however, are more apt than adults to respond to fever and infection with deliria and hallucinatory states. True hallucinations can also be seen in acute brain syndromes of children. But hallucinations in functional psychiatric disorders are extremely rare, most commonly found in children from backgrounds of multiple deprivations. [167]

Culturally endorsed sex differences must be recognized

in evaluating children.[61] Shyness as a camouflage for with-drawn behavior is more acceptable in the girl, whose psy-chopathology may be ignored or viewed as exaggerated normal behavior. In fact, in most studies on child psy-chopathology,[95] boys far exceed girls in sex frequency in the following conditions: tics, enuresis, learning and language disturbances, and functional psychosis. On the other hand, girls have more difficulty in separation–indi-vidualization, are more apt to be thumb suckers and school "phobics." Careful demographic studies are neces-sary to rule out the possibility that these sex differences are based only on cultural gender role differences.*

The psychiatrist's approach to the mental status exam-ination of children differs considerably from that of the examination of adults. The child psychiatrist is not "neu-tral" in his attitude or approach to his patient. He begins the psychiatric interview in an active, warm, and suppor-tive manner, and as the interview unfolds, he varies his activity and support in proportion to the responsiveness of the child. Usually, the less active the child, the pro-portionately more active is the psychiatrist. The more

---

* Sex characteristics are divided into primary (genito-urinary structure), secondary (physical features associated with pubertal changes), and tertiary (gender differentiated social and behavioral patterns). Tertiary sex characteristics have been described by Birdwhistell.[22] As gender sig-nals, at least for the adult, they include carrying angle of the arm, space between the thighs, and inclination angle of the pelvis. Shoulder set and muscular development are less reliable indicators of gender. Tertiary characteristics become during development gender signals in interper-sonal communications.
    Research in the ontogenesis of gender signals is needed.

stressful and disruptive the experience is for the child, the more supportive is the psychiatrist.

Although there can be little "standardization" of the examination procedure for children, the reproducibility of diagnostic results is surprisingly high. Beiser has observed that "with all the individual styles in use, it is remarkable that experienced clinicians tend to agree on the evaluation of behavior as regards diagnostic examination in child psychiatry." [9]

Prior to diagnostic evaluation of children, there should be some preparation of the child.[109] The child does not require elaborate or detailed preparation. It is enough for the parents, usually the mother, to tell the child: (1) the parents are concerned about an aspect of the child's behavior or capacity; they can identify the concern for the child in simple language. For example, a mother can say: "Dad and I are wondering what can be done about your taking things that don't belong to you." (2) A child can be told by his parents: "We will be going to see a special kind of doctor who talks to children about their worries." The child should be given the impression that the doctor wants to help children, can understand them, and is interested in listening to children. (3) The doctor has seen other children who have similar problems and worries. (4) The doctor knows a little about the child's problems and will certainly be able to do something to help the child if the child can tell him more. It is usually best to tell these simple things to the child on the morning of the visit. The less time between the parents' preparation of the child and the diagnostic visit, the less are the child's anxious expectations. The child should not be prepared by giving him extravagant promises of material things. The child should not be told that the child psychiatrist is a "talking doctor whom you don't have to be afraid of." The child should not be told that "Mother will be waiting just outside the office." The child must not be told that "Mother wants you to tell the doctor *everything*." If the psychiatrist takes the time to explain these preparations to the parents, he will be reasonably certain that salient information can be derived from the child's fantasies of the visit and his distortions of the purpose of the examination, as well as the child's view of his presenting problems.

Talking to children during the diagnostic interview is facilitated by certain techniques that maximize interaction. The use of play, repetition, general comments ("thinking out loud"), and questions, rhetorical or directed to a third person, often encourage the silent child to comment on his feelings and thoughts. Direct questions must be asked with tact. Compare: "Are you afraid of anything?" with "Sometimes all boys seem to get scared about some things. I was wondering what things might have scared you."

Talking slowly and deliberately is one of the first requisites of interviewing children. Children tend to hear verbs more acutely than other parts of speech. Liberal usage of parlance in the subjunctive enhances the child's desire to tell about himself and his experiences. The subjunctive mode is an invitation to fantasy through which actions or emotional states are made suppositional or imaginary. If the child is reticent, the following syntactical structure, for example, can be used: "Suppose you were to take someone to your house, and suppose you were going to show him some things there, what kinds of things might he see?" Compare this approach with "What is your house like?" The former kind of questioning allows the child some degree of emotional distance by adding a game-like quality to the question. The use of hyperbole in speech can at times capture a child's interest and prompt responses. Overstatement in the negative elicits corrections and elaborations.

Much has been written about the psychiatrist entering the child's world, and meeting the child at his developmental level. That a child's eye-view of the world is magnified with adults present is well known but often forgotten.[42] The child's perceptual viewpoint is scaled according to his development. The child cannot immediately accept an interested, supportive, but unknown adult into his world. The psychiatrist, however, can lessen but not entirely correct the interpersonal gap. The best child psychiatrist remains only a talented "impostor" until basic trust is established. For this reason, the psychiatrist should not try to speak like a child. Overusage of adult approximations of childlike speech puts the child on guard. Children do not want to be patronized by adults.

Playing competitive games in early contacts with the

child is best limited to games of chance rather than those of skill, since the child does not expect an adult to lose games of skill. If a game of skill is played, the psychiatrist should support the child's view of reality by playing to win. Some children relate more easily through games of chance and can demonstrate aggressive capacities, formerly held in reserve, when bolstered by success.

It is important for the child psychiatrist to have a flexible routine in his approach to children. Depending upon the child's response in the initial interview, support and structuring can be appropriately varied to the needs of the child. The evaluation of a child involves a comparison of the child to established age-expected norms and to other children examined in the psychiatrist's practice. If the psychiatrist's interviewing approach to all children remains relatively constant without sacrificing flexibility, the individual child's responses in the diagnostic situation can be comparatively judged.

The child mental status examination should identify areas of ego strength as well as ego weakness. Assessment of special skills or development is as valid descriptively as are their counterpart deficiencies. Exceptionally advanced areas of functioning may, and often do, coexist with lagging or frankly deficient areas of development. The age-appropriateness of the child's behavior must be kept in mind during the evaluation. The younger the child, the more important the examiner's knowledge of age norms. In the psychiatric evaluation of adults, social norms are usually the reference points for adaptive behavior. In children, a behavioral constellation can be assessed primarily from the standpoint of the developmental level at which the behavior appears. The psychiatrist, uncertain of developmental norms, will usually overestimate the degree of pathology. Commenting on this error, Gesell wrote that "psychiatry has derived its concepts largely from the psychopathology of the adult, and has been preoccupied with the interpretation and treatment of mental disease." [67] There has been, however, an increasing tendency among child psychiatrists to utilize normative developmental data and view child disorders as deviations from developmental and behavioral norms. At a 1964 conference on problems of diagnostic classification in child psychiatry, Langford remarked: "Everyone who is concerned with children stresses again and again the importance of having a developmental frame of reference. In summary, we could almost say that the clinical syndromes are shaped by chronological age and development, the level of the personality organization at a particular time and the dynamic equilibrium between the child and his environment." [98]

Mental status material tends to be more observational with preschool children and more verbal with latency children. The desired goal is to facilitate verbal responses from children of all ages; but especially with younger children, a large proportion of diagnostic material must be obtained from an assessment of the child's total behavioral response and coping process in the interview experience.[113] Frequently, a period of observation of the preschool child in a nursery school situation is beneficial. The psychopathology and developmental profile of the preschooler are most apparent in the milieu of the nursery schools, where peer interaction can be observed.

Interactions in the interview require more than passive recording of responses. The psychiatrist's participation leads to another level of empirical data. An interviewing event with an 8-year-old girl illustrates the need to question isolated findings. When asked to write her name, the little girl wrote it in mirror writing, going from right to left on the page. The psychiatrist said: "That is not the way to write your name, but it is a fine trick. Who taught you to write it that way?" The little girl cheerfully identified her older sister as her teacher, and proceeded to write her name in the ordinary manner.

The child mental status examination, we believe, cannot easily be converted into a simple behavioral rating scale that will equal or surpass the clinician's observational results. A rating scale can identify and qualify behavioral categories; it can be used effectively by nurses and other paramedical personnel, and, for large populations of patients, it is more expedient and economical than the traditional mental status examination.[127] But a behavioral rating scale is static; it does not go beyond what it gives, and it is fixed in time and space. A psychiatric examination of children must take into account rapid fluctuations in the child's level of maturation and coping behavior. No fixed maturational equilibrium exists in time or space for a child in a psychiatric interview. Young children can pass during an interview through levels of behavior within the space of a few minutes, going, for example, from independence to infantile demandingness. Quantitative and qualitative changes in a child's perception of self can vary greatly during an interview. Children's time sense, frustration tolerance, and regression rate vary in terms of development and psychopathology. The psychiatric interview is not a static slice of life. It is a measure of a child's coping process—his over-all integrative function—which involves timing and patterning of ego devices and strategies to deal with specific problems aroused by both internal and external stimuli.[113]

Children are easily influenced by suggestion. They seek acceptance more eagerly than adults. They are concerned about confidentiality in a way different from adults.[107] Often they are eager to relate events at home, but wary of maligning their parents or betraying their parents' confidence. Paradoxically, although guarded about their feelings and their relationships with parents which could threaten their security, children—especially 4- to 6-year- olds—are frequently "chatterboxes" about details of home life. They are willing and usually accurate informers concerning the activities of their parents and siblings, and they are storehouses filled with those things which adults consider private and confidential. If the child senses no threat to his security, he is oblivious of what constitutes privileged information. They cannot, however, be expected to reveal their "secrets" easily to a stranger. But their lack of sophistication unwittingly allows much of their private world to reveal itself.

The composition of the child psychiatrist's office is naturally less important than his competence as an observer of children. Yet it is a constant component, one among many, in the evaluation of the child. The psychiatrist sees most of his patients there. There are several situations, however, which require examination outside the office. Besides consultation with hospitalized children, psychiatric examination of physically handicapped children in their homes, emergency visits, and situations that require obervations away from the office are occasionally called for. It is, however, preferable to examine the child in the office. The child psychiatrist uses his office as a constant and familiar setting, an extension of himself, against which he measures the child's behavior.

Specific recommendations for the physical arrangement of the office must be tempered by the child psychiatrist's personality style, nature of his practice, and practical requirements. There are few practitioners of clinical psychiatry who see children exclusively. An office usually serves for adults as well. Ideally, a room is set aside for children, but actually, most child psychiatrists' office space has only a separate area for the study of children. The examining office should be large enough to permit certain procedures such as play actitivities and the neurological play examination, but not so large as to appear immense to the child. The child's eye-view of his surroundings must be kept in mind. The furniture should be at the child's eye level and not block his view of the window. A window seat of the dormer variety is ideal for a small child. If the window is hung high on the wall, a riser or a small chair should be approximately positioned. A room without windows or with drapes tightly drawn is not advisable.

Ideally, a short distance, perhaps ten to twenty feet, should separate the examining room from the waiting room.[101] Separation from the parents takes place in a few seconds along a corridor. The child should know the whereabouts of his parents, yet not feel their physical presence at close range. Noises such as coughing, turning the pages of magazines, or shuffling about in the waiting room do not usually intrude upon the child's awareness. The room should be well lighted and bright in wall color. Breakable objects like figurines or vases are best avoided. If a child does break or damage an object in the office, he should be reassured as to its replaceability. If the child returns for additional diagnostic study or treatment, the broken object should be repaired or replaced. Paintings hung in the office should not be of the nursery variety. Nursery primitives rarely reflect the physician's taste and may insult the child's self-estimation. Children often welcome and even comment on abstract art. A good-sized clock should hang on the wall, or should be visible to the child if it is placed on the desk. Younger children, according to their attention span, can be shown what the length of the interview will be by pointing out the position of the hands of the clock at the end of the interview. Structuring the time aspect of the interview for the child is helpful in reducing his anxieties about separation from his parents.

The psychiatrist should center his attention on the child's activities and productions. Note taking during the interview is a hindrance to both observation and participation by the psychiatrist. And recording equipment should not be evident to the child. Children who spy dictaphones usually want to play with them. Some psychiatrists have tried to combine the child's investigative play with sample tape recordings by allowing the child to make recordings and then play them back. This technique may permit working through of material in treatment, but it is rarely of any value during diagnostic evaluation.

Sometimes a small mirror centrally placed is helpful in observing the child's behavior. It is better to have a small clothing rack in the office as well as in the waiting room. How the child removes his coat or sweater allows the psychiatrist an important glimpse into the child's self-help functions. It also reflects his preference for being held or touched. Overconcerned parents often make some remark about the child's clothing as the child separates from his parents.

The office should be equipped with a lavatory which the child can easily use. Running water is important in the office. A sink with soap, paper towels, and some cups is the center of certain play activities. A blackboard can be hung on the wall at a low enough height to invite drawing. Children often test the boundaries of permissible activity in the psychiatrist's office. They frequently want to play with the telephone, draw chalk lines on the wall, spill water, and keep the door open. General guidelines for permissiveness must take into account the child's view of the psychiatrist as a responsible adult. The child psychiatrist may play with the child, but he should never abnegate his adult responsibility.[82] His failure as an adult to lend any ego to a child during a diagnostic interview would warp the interaction and attendant observations. On the other hand, excessive permissiveness which aims at allaying the child's fear actually increases it.

If there is not a separate room for the examination and play activities of the child, then a portion of the consulting room should contain children's furniture. Most of the furniture in the room should be arranged peripherally, so that a central area is a free space for walking, throwing a ball, playing other games, and accommodating special examination techniques. The furniture should include a small wooden table and chairs, a toy shelf with supplies, and a blackboard. The chairs should be sturdy, so that the psychiatrist can join the child across the table. Elaborate watercolors, finger paints, and easels take more of the interview time than their diagnostic value merits. The contents of the toy shelf are important. The child psychiatrist should rely chiefly on sturdy and instructive play utensils, which give expression to the child's imaginative and creative abilities. Leftover projects from other children's diagnostic interviews or therapy sessions should not be displayed. If children, however, do notice these materials, a discussion about peer relations can be inaugurated.

The contents of the toy shelf are divided into raw materials and play originals.[8, 43] Raw materials include pencils, crayons, paper, paste, blunt scissors, paper clips, clay or "playdough," rulers, wooden blocks, pipe cleaners, and balloons. Play originals include a doll family, a small train, and other sequential vehicles which can be linked together, a few puppets, plastic soldiers or cowboys and Indians, dart gun, magnets, and a pack of cards. Small balls, pick-up sticks, and jacks are useful in assessing fine movement and coordination. More extensive play material presents a welter of choice to the child, wastes diagnostic time, and allows the child to take flight into recreational play. Furthermore, children who have been well informed by parents about the purpose of their visit to a child psychiatrist are often taken aback by a room filled with elaborate toys.

No attempt should be made to hide the child psychiatrist's identity as a physician. The office itself need not be called a "playroom." Informal attire is hardly a prerequisite for establishing rapport with children. The child should be told that the psychiatrist has met his parents and will be talking with them later. Waiting-room consultations with parents immediately after the psychiatric examination of the child are not advised, particularly if the child is present. The psychiatrist should greet the parents at the end of the interview and tell them that he will be in touch with them shortly.

If the psychiatrist's understanding of the child's mental and behavioral state is incomplete at the end of the initial interview, the child can be seen again. Examinations beyond two to three sessions, however, are rarely necessary unless the clinical picture is a mixture of overlapping etiologies. Multiple examinations for the purpose of gaining additional diagnostic data are ill-advised, particularly if the evaluating child psychiatrist plans referral for treatment. It is not a technical fault of the diagnostic process or of the psychiatrist's skill to have fallen short of dynamic and etiological diagnoses; occasionally diagnosis can be achieved only in treatment. A nonverbal and uncooperative child may be reached and later understood only in therapy.

The mental status examination for children may be divided into two broad areas of investigation. The first area is developmental, both phenomenological and psychodynamic. The second area is transectional and descriptive, and requires the deliberate, thoughtful participation of the psychiatrist in an evocative role with the child. Particular attention is given to general appearance, motility, coordination, speech, intelligent function, modes of thinking and perception, emotional reaction, manner of relating, fantasies and dreams, and character of play. The parts of the mental status examination are not performed or observed consecutively. Some of them overlap; most of them present themselves simultaneously during the examination. The arrangement of the subsections of the child mental status is a conceptual guide to the interviewer and should not be construed as a graduated approach to the child.

4.

A mental status examination for children

1. SIZE AND GENERAL APPEARANCE

Psychiatrists are so accustomed to going immediately beyond phenomenological data that they sometimes let their observational skills lie dormant. Frequently, clinicians show a mistrust of easily gathered phenomenological information. The child psychiatrist, in particular, must train himself to notice many surface phenomena and then proceed to understand such phenomena dynamically and developmentally.

The child's physical appearance must be carefully examined. Is the child large or small for his age? Is there evidence of retarded or accelerated physical development? Does the head seem large or small in circumference? Are there any facial features suggestive of endocrinopathy, congenital defect, metabolic error, or chromosomal abnormality? Hairline, set of eyes, tongue size, ear and nose cartilage formation, structure of teeth, and expression of the eyes all come within the examiner's purview. The examiner should ask himself questions about the child. Does the child remain in one place, or does he keep shifting and turning and twisting his hands? Does he bite his lip, twist his mouth, or suck his thumb? Is he a nail biter? Is there a fixed grin on the child's face? Does he pick at his skin, face, or genitals, and does he pull out his hair? Does the child walk on tiptoe? Does he have a "nervous" giggle?[144]

General nutritional status is easily assessed. Is the child cachectic, robust, or obese?[144] Does the child appear ill? Skin features to be noticed include coloring, evidence of vasomotor instability (including blushing and excessive perspiration), scars and bruises, hirsutism, rashes and excoriations. Excessive bruising, most marked over the extensor surface of the extremities, should alert the examiner to the possibility of inflicted trauma. X-rays of the long bones may reveal multiple linear fracture of varying ages, evidence of the "battered child" syndrome.[65]

Nail biting, thumb sucking, teeth gritting, hair pulling, and lip licking often leave unmistakable signs. Hypersalivation and drooling, muscular tension or flaccidity, tics, habit spasms and tremors, belching or hiccoughs, persistent yawning or stretching, and the continuum of alertness—somnolence—all come within the examiner's scrutiny. Respiratory signs of breath holding or hyperventilation may be present. Automatic activity, transient lapses of consciousness, and other signs of seizure activity may be evident. At times masturbation may be mistaken for epileptic activity.[60] Does the child act confused or perplexed? Is he incontinent? Cardiovascular signs of anxiety are manifest in carotid pulsations.

Beyond these immediately observable phenomena, other findings can be elicited by asking the child about his body. The child can be asked: "If I were your family doctor, and gave you an examination, what might I find?" In his psychiatric and physical examination, Levy asks children questions about form, function, and disability of body parts.[103] He finds that children are usually willing to talk about their physical attributes and are remarkably perceptive about small defects, particularly cosmetic ones, which would escape the attention of most clinicians.

Proceeding to another level of observation, the child's habitus, body care, and dress are appraised. Are his clothes clean? Is the clothing appropriate for the weather, age, and sex of the child? Does the child use gestures? An estimate of the child's sex-role identification and gender preference should be made. Clues to the gender-role preferences of the child are style of dress, speech, gestures, actions, posture, and hair style.[22, 114, 115] If there is notable blurring of sex-appropriate appearance, further history and projective psychological tests, especially human figure drawings, may be necessary for a more complete evaluation of gender role and gender signals.[22]

The examiner should notice which sensory modalities are used preferentially. Does the child keep feeling the forms of objects within his reach? Does he smell everything he picks up? Does the child remain at a distance, watching and listening, or, on the other hand, is he more inclined to finger, mouth, taste, and smell objects in the playroom? Often children will bring objects with them to the interview. The contents of a little girl's purse or a boy's pocket can indicate many facets of personality. The psychiatrist should ask himself in what respect the child's appearance is appealing.

Evidence for or against a child's alleged symptoms, gathered in advance through parents' reports, should be recorded. The psychiatrist remains alert to reported symptoms and appraises whether there is parental bias, distortion, or omission. Gender role, social maturity, regressive pull, and physical appearance are some of the "intangibles" that can be crucial in diagnostic appraisal and treatment planning.

Clinical Example:

Laura, a large and pretty girl, separated promptly from her mother and took a seat across from the psychiatrist, settling gracefully into a pose. Her straight blond hair was cut so that it hung over her forehead, long enough at times to obscure her vision. She managed to see by pushing her hair to the side, a movement repeated many times in the interview. Her skirt length was well above the knees, and she tugged at it to hold her skirt down over her crossed knees. Her lean and willowy body did not suggest the onset of puberty. She carried a large handbag and produced a wallet full of photographs of her contemporaries, mostly boys. Although she wore no make-up, her fingernails were painted a pale pink. Her voice was husky, and she smiled coquettishly. A large charm bracelet jingled as she gesticulated with bold strokes. When she talked about her cats and her fifth-grade studies, her thinking betrayed her appearance as a socially precocious ten-year-old. Her assumed mannerisms fell away as she voiced her primary concerns. Her former "poise" was a hostile caricature of adult feminine mannerisms, which mocked her mother, a successful actress.

2. MOTILITY

So many children are referred to psychiatrists because of hyperkinesis that it is incumbent upon the examiner to assess routinely the child's patterns of motoric activity. Hyperkinesis is found most commonly in boys of the early school years. The first task of the examiner is to identify those children whose motor behavior is a symptom of organic dysfunction, as in choreatic and postencephalitic conditions. In his referrals, the pediatrician or family practitioner will usually identify the majority of hyperkinetic children. Nevertheless, some hyperactive children, recognized only as disciplinary problems, come to the child psychiatrists for therapy.

The timing of the hyperactivity—whether it is random or purposive—calls for the examiner's patience and persistence in his observations. Artifacts such as a child's full bladder, medication, and fatigue should be ruled out. Does the hyperkinesis occur episodically? Is it associated with perseverative activity? Does it occur at random, or is it triggered by anxiety? Is it correlated with short attention span and low tolerance for frustration? Does it occur in the context of impulsive and uninhibited behavior?

Often children who appear to be motorically "driven" can play the following game: "Let's pretend you're in the army and have to follow orders. The first order is for you to sit as still and quietly as you can for two minutes— let's start now." Children with organically based hyper-motility have no tolerance for this game.[128]

If the child can play this game, the second task is to understand the hypermotility in terms of its dynamic meaning and the child's level of maturation. The appearance of rocking, tapping, swaying, head rolling, hair twirling, or nail biting, as well as other kinds of fidgeting, often is directly related to the examiner's questions. Such inner-stimulated activity is classified as purposive if it subserves a psychological need. Repetitive tic-like movements, usually rapid and transient, are differentiated from habit spasms.[140] Partial remnants of masturbatory or regressive patterned activity such as scratching, lip licking, pelvic thrusting, and repetitive leg movements may be increased with anxiety. An unstructured situation, like free play, may potentiate the movement or mannerism.

Persistent and nonpurposive outer-stimulated activity often accompanies organic deficit. This hyperactivity is most identifiable by the fact that it cannot be significantly altered by the psychiatrist's active intervention. Primary organic hypermotility, however, may have an element of psychogenic hyperactivity added to it. Further attempts are made to separate organic and neurotic components of hyperactivity on the basis of whether the motoric discharges are goal-directed and appropriately related to the child's perceptions. The neurotic hyperactive child asks how long the interview will last and is often concerned about what he is supposed to be doing, and he appears anxious about the psychiatrist's impressions and intentions. The organic hypermotile child, on the other hand, may appear unconcerned about the length of the interview and not unduly anxious about its meaning and implications for him.[153]

Hypokinesis must similarly be investigated. Is it accompanied by slowness in thought and speech? Is it related to dysphoric feelings? Is it part of a somnolent state with altered sensorium? Is it a companion to caution and timidity? The child psychiatrist first observes the prevalent over-all behavior and affect of the hypokinetic child, then attempts to interest and coax him into motoric activity. The failure of the child to respond to this encouragement helps to rule out the possibility of reticence, withdrawal, apathy, and anxiety as major determinants of the hypermotility. Some children respond to unfamiliar situations with hypomotile behavior. For instance, a couch in the office can suddenly become a bed and the setting for regressive, oppositional, or provocative behavior.

Clinical Example:

John, a 7-year-old boy with a shock of hair falling over his brow, came along slowly to the office, pausing to tie his shoelace on the stairs. He sat in the chair for the greater part of the interview. His hands were kept in his trouser pockets much of the time and he occasionally flipped his head back to toss the hair away from his eyes. His elbows and knees formed acute angles. His feet pointed back under the chair. The jaw muscles moved rhythmically as he drew a careful crayon picture of his family. Although his body showed minimal gross movements, muscular tension of major opposing muscle groups was evident. At the conclusion of the interview he sprang from the chair, ran down the stairway out of the building, and jumped around in the snow. He threw snowballs and waded in deep snowdrifts. He actively evaded his mother, who was trying to fasten the chinstrap of his cap. John had been relatively still during the interview, but his parents' report of his hyperactivity was confirmed by muscular tension during the interview and its sudden release at the end. There was purposive control and release to John's activity. There was none of the random restlessness that often accompanies low-threshold motorically driven children.

3. COORDINATION

Motoric abilities and perceptual motor skills represent more than neurological function in that they are also determined by learning and socialization. In a psychiatric interview, a child is rarely systematically tested for these skills. There are many opportunities for observing the child's motoric capacity.

Observation of the child's coordination begins in the waiting room; posture, gait, balance, and associated movements can be appraised when first meeting the child and further observed as the child goes to the playroom, as well as throughout the interview. The child's ascent and descent of a flight of stairs often provide valuable information, especially important in evaluating younger children. Two steps per stair, holding onto railings, and slowness or hesitancy in movements are clues which may signify coordination difficulty. The mildly neurologically impaired child may require structural supports in walking, such as the psychiatrist's hand, a railing, or the boundaries of a wall along a corridor.

The bulk of the data collected about fine motor coordination is accumulated during play activities. Is the child smooth, adept, and graceful in play activities? Girls who appear awkward can demonstrate excellent perceptual-motor function in a game of jacks or "Pick Up Sticks." Other simple games can be used for a rough appraisal of coordination. Boys who can throw and catch two small balls alternately with the doctor cannot be severely handicapped. Likewise, coordinated younger children can easily manipulate clay or link small objects such as paper clips.

Coordination always involves associated movements. Children should be observed during physical activity for graceful complementary movements. Is there awkward arrest of associated muscle groups, or spilling over of non-balancing and non-contributory muscular activity? Reciprocal movements, particularly of the hands, in which the contralateral hand at rest mirrors the movement of the active hand, represent a form of neurological disturbance. The child psychiatrist should observe the hands of the child for difficulties in fine movements and coordination. The natural ability of the child to transfer objects from one hand to the other, the development of prehension versus awkward palming, and the positioning of the fingers at rest or in activity provide information about coordination function. A young child can be handed a wrapped stick of chewing gum and then asked to unwrap and divide the stick while the examiner observes the digital performance required. The examiner must be aware that the awkward child may be apraxic[76] (Chapter 5).

The way a child makes a fist tends to differ by gender, the boy being more apt to flex the thumb and oppose the tip to the knuckle of the third finger. Girls tend to keep the thumb in extension when making a fist or they fold it under the second and third fingers. Frequently, a boy who makes a fist like a girl has difficulty in throwing a ball gracefully.[69]

The psychiatrist, knowing from the parents' history the handedness of the child in advance of the interview, observes hand preference and extent of ambidexterity. As Monroe notes, opposite hand-and-eye dominance may be an impediment to coordination of directional responses.[112] Cross-dominant children often display language disorders.[40] The psychiatrist can test for eye dominance by giving a rolled paper "telescope" to the child and noting which hand the child uses in taking the paper and which eye is used for sighting. For the purpose of the mental status examination, a brief excursion into the problem of dominance usually suffices if the child proves to have neither reading, writing, nor speech problems. If these disturbances do exist, additional diagnostic information can be obtained through referral to a language disorder specialist or clinic.

At some time in the interview all children should be asked to write or draw. A blackboard in the playroom provides space for the child and minimal structure. On the other hand, pencil and paper give permanent documents that can be useful for follow-up records. The examiner notes how the child manipulates the chalk or pencil and also whether the child turns his head and the paper while drawing. The psychiatrist should know the geometric figures that can be easily drawn by children at various ages. A 3-to-4-year-old child should be able to copy a circle, a 5-year-old a cross, and a school-age child a diamond.

Suspected perceptual-motor difficulties are more carefully adjudged in a modified Bender-Gestalt test. Children can be asked whether they can successfully ride bicycles, effectively swim, and perform various calisthenics without falling. Often the minimally uncoordinated child will tell the psychiatrist that he cannot field grounders well, catch fly balls, or win at hopscotch. In such situations, the psychiatrist should test further for neurological impairment. To allay the child's apprehension and maintain his cooperation, the neurological examination can be easily incorporated into a play atmosphere. Games of "Follow the Leader" and "Simon Says" turn the Romberg test and tandem gait testing into fun for the child. There are other games, useful for neurological examination, described in Chapter 5.

4. SPEECH

The appraisal of the child's speech requires more than listening for articulation defects. Verbal behavior entails speaking, reading, writing, spelling, and composition. Each component is an important part of linguistic behavior; each expresses, singly or in combination, a language dysfunction such as dyslalia, word-deafness, word-clutter, or a reading disorder.[40][41][50][112][119] Language dysfunction in the child is usually related to either brain damage or neurophysiological immaturity of the perceptual-motor apparatus.[26][130] Frequently there is a family history of language disturbance, either of reading, writing, or spelling. Thus motility is considered along with speech. Is the child hyperkinetic and overreactive to environmental stimuli? Can the child separate individual muscle groups? Does he have good gross motor control? The child's perceptual capacity must also be considered. How well does he draw a human figure? Is it commensurate to his chronological age according to Goodenough's norms? Does the figure demonstrate the child's spatial competence? What does the human figure reveal about his fine motor coordination, about his body image and body concept?

The child's spacial organization is also assessed in terms of lateral dominance. Does the child have residual ambilaterality? Does he reverse in reading, writing, or speaking? Figure-ground organization can most easily be appraised by use of the Strauss-Lehtinen Cards which have figures embedded in a strongly structural ground. The child's ability to differentiate between figure and ground is essential for later reading and speech.

Speech evaluation is usually divided into two areas for investigation: (1) the child's receptive capacities and (2) his expressive ability and output. With regard to the former, a determination should be made of the child's ability to hear the examiner, recognize the words, and understand what is said. For instance, a child may have borderline auditory acuity which can be tested by lowering the voice. The child may have impairment of attention which is tested by talking in a manner in which words are not emphasized. In addition, the child can be asked to reproduce a tapped-out pattern of sound as a test of auditory discrimination.

Once it has been established that the child hears, listens, discriminates, and relates to people, his capacity to understand is examined. A child must have age-appropriate concept adequacy in order to participate in meaningful conversation. Mental deficiency, language barriers, and rarely receptive aphasia lower the child's concept adequacy. Some children, particularly prelatency children, may understand simple phrases that are presented in isolation, yet seem baffled by the same phrases when they are couched in complex sentences. A child may respond to part rather than to whole sentences. If the child is asked: "Which kinds of games do you like to play with your friends when you come home from school?" he may respond to part, all, or none of the question. He may be able to respond to the entire three parts of the complex query if it is subdivided: "Which games do you like?" "Whom do you play them with?" and "When do you play them?" Children who have difficulty in comprehension because of conceptual disturbances can be evaluated more meaningfully after disorders of reception and expression are ruled out (see Section 6).

The child's expressive language is evaluated in terms of quantity and quality. Is the child verbose or laconic? Does the child talk incessantly? Does he lisp? Is his speech articulate? Is his speech slow and punctuated with pauses? Does the child's speech make sense to the examiner? Is his speech accompanied by substitutive or non-verbal communication?

Mutism is either essential or "elective." Mutism must be differentiated from expressive aphasia. Initially in the interview mutism does not necessarily pose a total barrier to the examiner. Will the child whisper? Perhaps he will talk after he is given a glass of water, or after he is reassured that the parent is present in the waiting room. Perhaps the mute patient will signal assent or denial by shaking his head and then verbalize in order to clarify communication. He may at first read aloud. The psychiatrist can often elicit speech by singing nursery rhymes or familiar songs, then deleting the last word and looking expectantly at the child for a response. This maneuver is effective with both autistic and aphasic children. In the former, it maintains enough distance in interpersonal relations to allow for participation. In the latter, it presents a cue for rote response.

The child's verbal output is characterized by articulation, rhythm, rate, organization, and syntax. What is the quality of the voice? Is it harsh, hoarse, breathless, or nasal? Is the pitch too low, too high, fluctuating, or monotonous? Is it well modulated in volume? Does it fade? Articulating defects are evaluated in terms of their severity and constancy. Severity is judged according to the number of articulation defects in speech as well as by their adverse effect on intelligibility. Many children can produce sounds in isolation, but their articulation does not remain clear when they are burdened with the need to relate a complicated thought sequence that requires patterning and structuring. Children with articulation difficulties clearly show this pattern when asked to report a story. The pattern of articulation errors is related to the content of speech and its possible psychodynamic importance. If a child's articulation errors imitate infantile speech ("baby talk")—a dyslalia of lisping and slurring accompanied by disjointed grammar—the speech is usually accompanied by other evidence of regressive behavior. Infantile speech is often the child's concept of "baby talk" rather than an accurate reproduction of primitive speech. For example, a 5-year-old boy who was reacting to the birth of a sibling said: "Johnny [referring to himself] do pitchers Mommy like for drawing." Older children with articulation or phonetic defects sometimes have structural defects such as lingual or palatine abnormalities. Focal CNS damage producing dysarthria is rare in children. A frequent cause of dysarthria in children is drug toxicity.

Dysrhythmias of speech, like stuttering, are evaluated for their psychodynamic and maturational significance. Age-appropriate norms are essential for the evaluation. Stuttering of a 3-to-4-year-old whose thoughts outpace his tongue, for example, is not unusual. Children who grope for "and," "um," and "ah" in spaces between words are rarely blocking. Children who seem to struggle for words, especially common nouns, should be tested for expressive aphasias. This is done simply by asking them to name common objects in the playroom (see Chapter 5).

The rate of speech largely varies in direct proportion to intelligence. Pressure of speech in children is almost always accompanied by a rise in pitch. Bursts of rapid speech are not unusual. Scanning speech raises questions of CNS damage or degeneration, which, if present, is usually accompanied by other motor disturbances. Pitch is helpful in estimating a child's anxiety. Anxious children frequently speak with tight voices. There is a special type of high-pitched, whining speech which is often produced by severely ego-impaired children. It is characterized by a piping monotony. The monotony of the child's voice, unwavering and unalterable, is often paralleled by the stereotypy of his responses to other children and adults. Monotony is also a part of the developmental language disturbance of dyslalic and dyslexic children.

The organization of speech into syntax and concept formation is age-related. Impairment can occur on the basis of many pathological conditions.[93] There may be fragmentation of thought, overinclusiveness or running together of separate ideas. The clanging, rhyming, or playful manipulation of words is usually benign in preschool children. Uncommunicative humming, rhyming, or seemingly playful word distortions in latency and pubescent children can be either autistic or oppositional. Echolalia must be differentiated from simple mimicry. Persistent echolalia can represent repeating in the service of clarification. In this case the child struggles to communicate through an expressive aphasic disorder. Echolalia is also seen in autistic children, where its dynamic function is to mock. Gross misuse of pronouns and gender can signal serious ego disorder. The persistent reversal of pronouns in person and gender, as well as the inability to speak in other than the present tense, in children over the age of 5, when not accompanied by difficulty in object relations, suggests organic brain damage or mental retardation.

5. INTELLECTUAL FUNCTION

The child psychiatrist's task in assessing intellectual function requires only that he be able to make an estimate as to whether the child is average, deficient, or exceptional in intellectual resources.[102] This estimate is not a measurement; it is merely a clinical impression. The child psychiatrist tries to define existing cognitive function rather than potential capacity. Gross deficit, as well as special talents, is clinically easily determined. The bright, well-informed child is quickly recognized. He is usually verbal, widely interested in his environment, and quick to respond to the examiner's suggestions and queries. Vocabulary, comprehension, and quality of communication are usually proportional to the level of intellectual function. Creativity, spontaneity, and social poise are indicative of, among other things, higher intellectual function, but their absence does not necessarily indicate a mediocre I.Q.[37]

A rough guide to the level of intelligence in younger children is their ability to identify their body parts. Three-year-old children should have basic knowledge about facial features and major limb parts. The 5-year-old should be able to identify wrist, ankle, elbow, and knee. The 7-year-old usually recognizes such body parts as jaws, temple, forearm, and shin. Sophistication in anatomic information is reflected in greater detail by figure drawings.

Memory is a poor measure of intellectual function in children, particularly for children that parrot well in response to parents and teachers who highly value rote learning. Long attention span and concentration are again positive indicators of intelligence. Yet impairment of these functions in children does not necessarily imply mental retardation or deficiency. The psychiatrist should reserve his opinion of the child's cognitive function, if the child appears on careful examination more intellectually compromised than his general appearance and behavior would suggest. Then a thorough evaluation, including psychometrics, is warranted. Kanner has reminded us that negativism, emotional blocking, regressive withdrawal, and special sensory receptor impairment can mask the child's intellectual potential.[91]

The clinical evaluation of a child's intellectual functioning must rely heavily on observation of behavior and performance. One of the behavioral signs of intelligence is the performance to conclusion of goal-directed tasks. If the child announces that he will pursue a task, perhaps demonstrating a learned skill, the psychiatrist notes whether the task is performed well, is carried to a conclusion, and is independently conducted. If the child asks for assistance, the psychiatrist has the option of suggesting new pathways which challenge the child's learning capacity. Children who respond to new suggestions in a negative fashion, citing old methods of doing things as their directing force, may be either restricted in their capacities for learning or oppositional in their behavior. The former possibility is often borne out by complementary evidence of an intellectual ceiling in which the child turns to preferred tasks in an effort to demonstrate other capabilities. The latter possibility is echoed in other demonstrations of ritualistic or negativistic behavior, as seen in the manner of relating and modes of thinking and perception.

The common clinical finding of maturational lag can misleadingly suggest low intellectual functioning. The child psychiatrist must often attempt an estimate of social intelligence, particularly important in the diagnosis of the understimulated child. Questioning the child about games played with peers, places he has visited or lived in, current preferences in toys or television programs, can provide information helpful in differentiating between the socially unexposed and the mentally retarded child.

Psychometrics are, of course, most sensitive in the determination of intellectual functioning. Nevertheless, the psychiatrist should attempt a clinical estimation of intelligence. In three clinical situations, however, the clinician is at an advantage in gauging intellectual function. The first is the preschool child for whom formal measurement of intelligence more closely approximates a neurological examination. The second involves the minimally verbal or depressed child whose performance and speech are inhibited. The third concerns the grossly disturbed child whose psychotic disorganization distorts intellectual function, while leaving intact islands of ego function. The psychiatrist should try to identify the areas of relatively intact ego function.

Clinical Example:

A 7-year-old girl who had been placed in a series of foster homes had repeated the first grade and was failing the second grade. She gave little of herself in the initial part of the interview. Her answers to most questions were: "I don't know." At other times, she sat silent, hunching her shoulders. Her answers to questions asked contained inaccurate information and seemed forced. She was, however, easily engaged in play. But her free-play activities were young for her age. She made a clay doll, poured water from one cup to another, and drew primitive pictures of animals. When she misspelled elementary words on the blackboard, she explained this by saying: "I don't care . . . what's the difference?"

When she was asked what she thought was the purpose of the interview, she at first said that she did not know; but when she was asked to guess, she replied: "Oh, you're probably going to send me to another house." When she was assured that this was not likely, she corrected the earlier misspellings and cooperated in talking about herself. The interview experience was reproduced in psychometric testing. When tested earlier by the school psychologist, her full scale I.Q. was 73; after the interview, it was 102.

6. MODES OF THINKING AND PERCEPTION

When the child begins school his thinking is then the verbalization of his mental processes. Until that time, his thinking had been mainly expressed through the motor apparatus. The school-age child comes to rely on speech to express thought. Still he remains largely egocentric and for a while can handle only one idea at a time. During latency, however, his conceptual style and ability change, the Piagetian progression of which the child psychiatrist should know.[110, 124]

The child's ego-defensive mechanisms and ego style can be discerned through observing the prevailing behavioral attitudes of the child. The child defends against unconscious material with more global avoidance and denial than an adult. Adults block, but children balk. There is less separation between primary and secondary process thinking in children. The child's anxiety can become very real. But some children, particularly those with obsessive or phobic mechanisms, can talk about their anxiety. With children, hallucinations, delusions, overinclusive thinking, word salads, and neologisms are often difficult to identify.[3] They can be misleading in their clinical and developmental significance. Age-specific norms, social class, and subcultural standards must be taken into account. For instance, Wilking and Paoli have demonstrated the importance of socioeconomic factors in understanding hallucinations in nonschizophrenic children. They found considerable differences between hallucinations in schizophrenic and nonschizophrenic children. In the latter group ". . . the presentation is orderly and the content related to reality . . . [hallucination of the nonschizophrenic children] represent an uneasy but reality-oriented balance between the expression of libidinal and aggressive drives, ego functions, adaptive mechanisms, and attempts at superego controls.

The schizophrenic child expresses the extent of his ego disorganization in his hallucinations." [167]

The child's tendency to express at times seemingly bizarre thoughts must be distinguished from an inability to differentiate between primary and secondary process thinking. For example, the psychiatrist can ask: "I know you call these rockets, but what do you really know them to be?" Some children hold on to silly phrases or primitive conceptual modes because they have learned that these annoy adults. What seemed at first blush bizarre may be oppositional or provocative. The availability of fantasy material in the interview, especially if it is not related to play activities, provides a clue to the child's capacity for containment of dereistic thought. Fantasies are evaluated in terms of whether they are vivid, immediate, structured, repetitive, and pleasurable. Vivid and frightening fantasies are usually accompanied by pressure of speech or histrionic display. Peculiar fantastic verbalizations should be examined for their origins. They often become more dynamically comprehensible once questions of "Where did you hear that?" or "Who said that?" are asked.

The child's concepts of time, space, and body image are age-specific and indicate the developmental rate of the child. For example, a 3-to-4-year-old child rarely considers his small size and limited capabilities, whereas a 9-to-10-year-old youngster is painfully aware of his limitations. The concept of death as a final and inevitable separation is not available to children under age 8; yet their concepts of time and space are expanded compared to that of the adult.

Unlike the adult who can be asked about time, place, and person in a psychiatric examination, the child's orientation is largely determined by his ability to communicate appropriately with the examiner. Often children who are asked early in the interview where they are and who the examiner is respond only with vacant stares. Some of them have been told extravagant stories by parents about the psychiatrist's playrooms full of toys or his special evaluative tasks. But many parents tell their children precisely the information which the psychiatrist has directed prior to the child's interview. Most children gather from the interview that they have been talking to and playing with a doctor who is interested in their "problems." The best that can be expected for the pre-school child's orientation is his ability to synthesize the experiences of the interview. Rather than asking a child where he is, the psychiatrist asks for age-appropriate descriptions of what has happened during the interview. The use of formal, adult-patterned mental status questions often meets with disbelief and contrary response from children. The proximity of children's thinking to primary process, concretizing thought does not allow them to cooperate passively, but rather stirs up their recently revised paleological thinking. As one child put it in an interview: "That doctor asked me where I was. He must be crazy."

The child's self-concept is elicited in response to questions of why he is coming to see the doctor or what he would like the doctor to change or have changed himself. Predominant identification models and ego-ideals help point to the child's self-concept. Questions of favorite journeys and the preferred people the child would take along can indicate the child's models for identification. Discussion of matters of bodily form and function elicits the child's body image and body percept. Magic wishes may tell something about concerns, desires, and hopes.

Egocentric thought is the rule with prelatency children. Counter-phobic expressions are also commonplace. Bragging and extravagant claims call attention to phobic undercurrents. Human reference and the ratio of animate to inanimate objects in speech and fantasy should be noted. Some young children can talk about themselves; others, only through projective reference to animals. Their ability to translate animal representations into human forms should be noted. The psychiatrist can translate for the child the latter's animal references into human terms, to the third person—and then observe whether the child follows his example.

Obsessive thinking in children, especially latency children, is commonplace. Its preponderance must be striking, or its effect cognitively paralyzing, for such thinking to be considered pathological at this age. The child who has a rigid way of expressing himself, who insists on completing his ideas, and who tries to control the interview, is frequently compulsive and manneristic in his play activities.

Children who appear suspicious of the psychiatrist's intentions, and express concern in regard to what will happen to them in the interview, are not necessarily paranoid. A prelatency child's caution with the more probing questioning of adults can reflect defensiveness and lack of trust, but these attitudes are rarely indicative of paranoid defenses or frank ego impairment. It is hardly paranoid for a small child not to trust a strange adult. Furthermore, the prelatency child tends to externalize his feelings. The externalizations, however, are fleeting and unsystematized as compared to paranoid projections. In addition, the child's concept of causality is determined by the level of conceptual development.[99] Until age 7 or more, animism is still part of a child's thinking, so that he attributes life to inanimate objects and cannot separate parts in a causal sequence.

On the other hand, pubertal and postpubertal adolescents are more apt to develop organized paranoid thinking. Harrison's study of paranoid children was largely based upon cases of pubertal adolescents—none younger than age 11.[80] Despert's findings also suggest that paranoid thinking, as reflected in delusions, appears only after puberty and is then less well organized than adult thought disorders.[45]

Circumstantiality and irrelevance are so common in children that they have little diagnostic significance. The child who repeatedly answers, "I don't know," should be invited to guess. Those who take flight into play can be asked to tell what they are thinking about.

Clinical Example:

An 8-year-old boy who had been referred with a chief complaint of restlessness and aggressive behavior used the strange word "honbeater" during the diagnostic interview. Although he had a squeaking, high-pitched voice, especially when agitated, there was no indication of an articulatory defect. His grammar was not bizarre. With inquiry it was learned that his speech was at times imitative of his mother's. She had once told him in anger: "You better not say that, hon, or I'll beat your head on the floor!" Later investigation proved that most of his other strange words and phrases were replicas of his parents' idiosyncratic speech rather than his own neologisms. His father would often say: "Silentium, desistium, knock-it-offibus," rather than "Stop it."

7. EMOTIONAL REACTIONS

The full spectrum of emotional reactions, with the nuances and subtlety characteristic of adults, is not available to children. Affectivity in young children is blunt and not well disguised. Prelatency children cannot easily dissimulate feelings. They rarely need to be encouraged to express their feelings. This is not the case with older children. School-age children have learned to temper and camouflage emotional outpourings. Indeed, their ability to control open aggression, giggling, whining, or crying is often equated with "maturity." The child psychiatrist finds himself in the position of inviting evidence of those reactions which the child is striving to master. In order to avoid iatrogenic overreaction, the psychiatrist approaches the area of a child's feelings with care and support and uses the evidence of stored feeling as demonstrated in the child's verbalizations, drawings, or play as points of departure for his clinical hunch. He compares the child's mastery over and depth of emotional response to age-graded norms and makes liberal allowance for the child's regressive potential. He also notes with interest the child's efforts to control an open breach of feeling or the coping mechanisms which are brought into play once the feelings have overwhelmed the child's poise. Often the healthier child shows more feeling—perhaps to the point of "emotionality"—but demonstrates resourceful coping mechanisms for recovery. The less healthy child with brittle control may not show so much feeling, but the psychiatrist is not advised to stress such a child for a glimpse at the emotional decompensation.

In older children, phrases put into the third person, such as "Sometimes a boy would feel sad about that," or, "I guess a girl could get angry when that happens," facilitate meaningful emotional responses. The most readily elicited emotional reactions are fear, anxiety, anger, sadness, and shame. Although these feelings are less disguised in children, special techniques are nevertheless sometimes necessary in order to elicit them. Affective states in children can be elaborated into secondary emotional responses such as apathy, petulance, arbitrariness, truculence, sulking, and docility. Once these secondary patterns are apparent, the psychiatrist should attempt to convert them through words and play back into their primary emotional roots.

Tearfulness and crying do not necessarily indicate sadness, particularly in preschool children. These responses can best be understood in relation to what has just transpired in the interview. Crying may be a signal of fear or the result of frustration; it may indicate overflow of mounting tensions. Girls display sadness more openly than do boys, who in turn more readily exhibit hostile and aggressive feelings.[156]

Appropriateness of affect is less assuredly determined in children than in adults. A child's smiling, ostensibly unrelated to humor or joy, does not necessarily signify inappropriate affect. Many children smile in response to fear and tension. There is a type of smile, however, that lingers on the child's face and is accompanied by an averted gaze. This so-called "inner smile" may be inappropriate, a harbinger of a serious emotional difficulty. Changes in affect during an interview are frequently greater in the prelatency child. A child's mood is variable and often follows fluctuating tension during the interview.

In an outline of a mental status for diagnostic interview, Chess refers to variations in affect during an interview. "In the course of an interview a continuous change in affect may be observed. If, after manifesting a restrained, shy, and apprehensive manner, a child becomes progressively more at ease during the interview, so that he appears relaxed and freely spontaneous when it ends, one may reasonably conclude that the final behavior is characteristic and that his initial conduct represented a reaction to his uncertainty and apprehension over a new situation. Assuming that this is the case, was the initial apprehension excessive?" Chess goes on to a consideration of the child who was so free and outgoing from the inception of the interview that the very lack of initial caution presented reason for further investigation.[32]

Quantitative and qualitative variations of mood must be assessed. Apathy, for example, should be gently probed for its tenacity, depth, and dynamic function. Apathy can be associated with withdrawal, mental retardation, deprivation syndromes, toxicity, and depression. As a measure of affective responsivity it is helpful to ask a child to tell a funny story or a joke, keeping in mind the age-specific qualities of children's jokes. Many angry children are only able to express this feeling through jokes. For instance, they may register glee in the failure of the psychiatrist to guess the answer to their riddle. Such "latency jokes" are well designed to mock the adult status and reassure the child.

Assessing the degree of anxiety in children is a special matter. In the adult psychiatric examination, the examiner is sensitive to the presence of anxiety in the patient and its precipitation. With children, however, the absence of anxiety concerns the examiners more. The prelatency child typically externalizes fears, most noticeably at ages 3–5. Free-floating anxiety in children is infrequent.[97] Externalized reaction of fear and dread is the rule. When a child speaks of "nervousness," he often is describing irritability or restlessness. Outside of nausea, vomiting, and tension headaches, a child rarely describes physiological concomitants to anxiety. A child's anxiety is more apt to be expressed physically through motoric activity. If there is a phenomenological difference between fear and anxiety in children, fearful children seem to retreat, either by hypomotility or by withdrawal, and anxious children appear to express this state either by hyperactivity, counterphobic bluffing, or by acting out behavior.

Clinical Example:

Sally, an 8-year-old girl referred for outbursts of crying and temper tantrums, seemed resigned to the interview as she came into the office. Her head was bent, and her eyes avoided direct contact. Her verbal responses were at first stereotyped. She answered most questions "I don't know," or "because . . . just because," while looking at her feet. She seemed to be struggling to control her feelings. This was most apparent as she spoke of coming to a psychiatrist "because my mother says I'm a problem."

Until that point, the interview had been labored, slow, and unproductive. Sally had no inclination to play or to talk spontaneously about herself. The examiner told her that he once knew "a little girl who did a lot of worrying and felt she couldn't find grown-ups who could understand these worries." Sally made no verbal response but looked directly at the psychiatrist for a brief moment. Taking the cue, the psychiatrist went on: "Sometimes this little girl would worry so much that she couldn't eat." "Oh, that's not me," said Sally. "What might you do?" Sally started fidgeting with the sash of her dress. The psychiatrist again asked: "What might you do if the worries get real big?" After further fidgeting and biting her lip, she said: "Nothing." Now more sure of his ground, the psychiatrist continued: "Well, I sense that you must be pretty worried right now." "How do you know?" she said. "Because you seem to be like this girl— maybe sad and holding back your feelings." Tears rolled down Sally's cheeks. The psychiatrist then said: "Maybe you can talk a little about what it's like to feel sad." Sally regained her composure, wiped the tears away, and said she would like to play. She then expressed some of the feelings about her mother.

8. MANNER OF RELATING

Manner of relating includes the degree of independence of the child and his blend of coping behavior. The capacity of the child to interact is observed commencing with the initial contact with the child in the waiting room. It is important to observe in detail the character of the child's separation from the accompanying parent. How the parent handles in turn the child's separation is noteworthy. Does the child come along easily? Does he look back to the parent for support and approval? Does the child extend his hand to the doctor, accept the doctor's offered hand, or "go it alone?" Do the child's formal expressions and actions indicate fearful anticipation of the approaching interview?

As the child draws closer to the psychiatrist during the interview, the latter has the chance to sample the child's usual coping patterns. The child who becomes overly familiar and chatty may use familiarity as a defense. Other children, after some initial reticence, may take over or take charge of the interview. Some may affect mock adult postures of relating. Others may appear to be "at home," thoroughly enjoying themselves. The child may be worried about confidentiality; and, if so, he may ask if the psychiatrist will talk to his parents. After gaining comfort and courage, some children will ask the psychiatrist what he thinks of him and what he plans for him. If the child can relate with any warmth at all, the psychiatrist will want to know whether there is a willingness to return on the part of the child. His questions may reveal an interest in returning to the psychiatrist. Frequently, children are interested in whether the examiner sees other children. This interest can be generated by sibling rivalry or by a desire to return to the psychiatrist.

Many preschool children will react to the strange circumstances of the interview by attempting to rejoin their parents. Some will dart out of the office to see if Mother is still there. Others will use a trip to the bathroom for similar purposes. For a small group of children, the interview can proceed only if the parents' physical presence is assured. With these children, the psychiatrist observes the counterpoint between the child-parent interaction and the child's relatedness to the examiner. Often a "weaning" situation results, with the child venturing forth in an ever increasing distance from his parents. The psychiatrist then watches for the mother's signals to the child, to see whether she encourages or sabotages the child's efforts.

Some children appear indifferent to the interview, but few demonstrate the indifference sometimes found in adults. Since the child psychiatrist is usually active in the first stages of the initial interview, the child's reaction to him can readily be observed in an unfolding continuum. It is usual for children to progress from distance and reserve to warmth and trust during the interview.

How the child addresses the psychiatrist is a clue to his manner of relating. He may avoid calling the examiner by any name, or he may call him "Doctor," "Mister," or use pronouns. As the child becomes comfortable, he usually settles on a role for the psychiatrist, unspoken but nevertheless communicated. The psychiatrist tries to identify his assigned role—be it teacher, friend, physician, disciplinarian, peer confidant, surrogate parent, protector, foe, or playmate. He observes whether the child looks at him when speaking or avoids visual contact. A child may need to communicate indirectly through drawings, doll play, written notes, play telephones, or the game "Let's Pretend."

Physical contact with prelatency children can be utilized to determine approach-avoidance behavior. This is best reserved until well into the interview. Does the child, first of all, stand close to the psychiatrist? Does he seem afraid that the psychiatrist may come close to him? Does he shrink back if the psychiatrist is next to him in the playroom? As the child becomes more relaxed in the interview, the psychiatrist can further evaluate the child's feelings about physical closeness. Does the child raise his arms as the psychiatrist lifts him from his chair? Does he seem to spurn physical contact and move farther away as the psychiatrist joins him at the play table or on the floor? Does the child welcome physical contact to the point of being coy or seductive? Some differences in response to the psychiatrist in the interview are age and sex specific. For instance, a 5-year-old child is usually more giving and trusting than a late latency child. The child's responses to the psychiatrist in terms of sex-typed behavior are important, particularly in the phallic period of development. Does the contrasexual child remain at a distance from the psychiatrist because of the sex difference?

Several other factors are helpful in the assessment of the child's ability to relate to the examiner. Is the child curious? Or is he aloof and diffident? Does the child require reassurance, praise, and encouragement? Or is he self-sufficient? Does the child tease and play games? Does he respond in a straightforward manner? Is there provocative clowning? Is the child negativistic and oppositional, or cooperative and even compliant? Is the child openly hostile and aggressive, or is he passive and inhibited?

Reality testing in the prelatency child is measured by the criteria of appropriate and adaptive behavior. Cognitive form and content are not readily helpful in evaluating reality testing unless the child is grossly psychotic. The child's capacity to respond and his style of response to the psychiatrist are most revealing of his reality testing. In addition, his coping behavior—a composite of affective, motor, and cognitive function in response to stresses of the interview—provides clues to the effectiveness of reality testing.

Clinical Example:

Harry, a 7-year-old boy, started the interview by going to the blackboard and writing "A, B, C." He seemed to be responding to internal stimuli. When he was asked his name, he took some clay and rolled out thin segments to spell "Peter Paul Almond Cluster." He had two brothers, Peter and Paul. His attention span was short-lived, and he often punctuated his activity with chants. He seemed at first to be oblivious of the psychiatrist's presence. A few responses unrelated to questions posed by the psychiatrist were made. If play activities were used with this boy, responses, if they occurred, were delayed. He was asked whether he wet the bed. (He was a persistent enuretic.) He gave no related response. When the tap water was turned on in the sink and he was again asked about bedwetting, he replied: "He doesn't do that." The water was then turned off, and he was asked: "Do you wet the bed sometimes?" He replied: "He never do that; I do." While drawing a picture, he said: "That's all

right . . . doing fine. . . . He's a good boy today."
When he looked in the direction of the psychiatrist, his
gaze was unfocused. He often walked into children's furniture. At the end of the interview he made the only contact with the psychiatrist when he took the chalk from
the psychiatrist's hand to write "The end" on the blackboard.

Harry could communicate occasionally, but only
through the most remote methods.

9. FANTASIES AND DREAMS

The fantasies and dreams of children are less distorted
than those of adults. Anna Freud regards children's
dreams as "certainly easier to interpret" because the child
stands closer to them than the adult.[63] The complex-
ity of dreams—their length, elaboration, and symboliza-
tion—varies directly with age. If the child is reluctant to
relate a dream in the interview, he can be encouraged to
draw a picture of the dream and then tell a story based
on the picture. It is common for 3-to-4-year-old children
to relate dreams as though they were reality experiences.
A child under the age of 7 assumes that dreams are not
part of the dreamer and that the events of a dream are
related to "creatures" or "people" who appear in the
dream. Not until the Piagetian phase of concrete opera-
tions, between ages 7 and 11, does a child regard dreams
as internal thoughts.[110] The more personalized and vivid
the dreams of older children, the greater the likelihood
of psychic disturbance. Phallic children replace early

dreams of "animals" with "monsters" and "witches"; in latency the content further changes. "Monsters" and "witches" become "enemy soldiers" or "Roman legions." Dreams and fantasies are also evaluated along the lines of content. The closer the content of the dream to the presenting symptoms—again adjusting for the factor of age—the more likely its pathological significance. The emotional feeling that accompanies the child's narration of dreams and stories must be considered in the clinical evaluation. For instance, some children are provocative "hams" and will tell fantastic stories based on their dreams with ease and relish.

There are several techniques which indicate the child's freedom to relate his fantasy life. Toward the end of the interview, or once the child is comfortable, he can be asked what he had imagined his experience with the doctor would be like. Often the child will then comment on the disparity between his preconceived notion of the interview and his actual experience with the doctor. The child's concept of body parts and functions, fantasies of physical injury and repair, and fantasies of what doctors do to children provide other data on the content and style of fantasy life. Most of these techniques are applicable to the neurotic child. In the obviously disturbed child, fantasies are so available and their content so transparent that there is little need to press the child for more details.

Clinical Example:

A 3-to-4-year-old child can tell a dream of, say, "a tiger was biting my leg," and describe his feelings, but a 6-to-7-year-old child who relates this dream with little affect may have an affective disturbance. Contrast these dreams given by two 8-year-old boys: "The Indians were firing on the soldiers in the fort. A big Indian raised his hatchet to scalp a soldier when all of a sudden it starts to rain, and all the fires were put out." The second child reported a dream: "My father put me and some of my cousins in a store where there was a big circle so that you could see down the road. That night my mother and father had a big fight. Then my father brought my mother to the store in a car. When I went down, I could see my father put my mother on the road and then he ran her down. I ran out of the store, screaming, 'Mommy.' "

The two dreams are apparently concerned with aggression. The former, however, allows for psychic distance and resolution; its success does not disturb psychic equilibrium. The second dream has little disguise or containment of affect. The first dream was related in an off-hand way. The second dream was narrated with anxiety and hyperactivity. It is not necessary to analyze these dreams in detail in order to estimate the relative ego organization of these two children. Furthermore, other areas of the mental status would substantiate the clinical impressions drawn from dream material.

10. CHARACTER OF PLAY

Some form of play is expected and should be encouraged in the psychiatric examination of all prepubertal children. Prephallic children play readily with amorphous objects, whereas older children tend to utilize structured play situations such as puppets, scenarios, and games. In general, however, the simpler the play materials, the greater the availability of dynamic material. Paper, pencils, crayons, clay, wood blocks, dolls, and puppets, along with a water supply in the office, make up the bulk of necessary materials for play.

All play activities should be observed for formal characteristics, including persistence, repetitiveness, ingenuity, age- and sex-appropriateness, competitiveness, orderliness, type of closure, and intensity.[23, 37]

Play is that part of the mental status examination which both facilitates and embellishes transactions between child and physician. The child who talks freely can be invited to play. And the child who plays easily can be urged to converse. Furthermore, play provides a panoramic view of the child.[104] What better method of observing fine motor coordination, intelligence, motility, speech, and fantasy is there than through the medium of play? The character of the play bridges the gap between the child's affects and perceptual-cognitive functions. In the diagnostic situation children are so close to unconscious material that they cannot readily communicate its derivatives. Yet they can often dramatize the material in play.[105] In the diagnostic context, the formal and configurational character of the play—how the child plays rather than what the content symbolizes—provides valuable information. At this point in the child's evolution play activity is equivalent to the manifest content of a dream. The psychiatrist does not intervene at this stage of the play activity. Later, if the child is in therapy, the psychiatrist can guide or structure the child's play activity to elaborate dynamic themes. The psychiatrist's intrusions at the time of the diagnostic interview, however, can produce misleading artifacts. In the initial interview, therefore, the psychiatrist should encourage free play.[159] If structured play is used at all in the initial interview, it should be reserved until the end of the interview for the purpose of testing a dynamic hypothesis that the psychiatrist has made from material obtained from the parents' history and the child's free play.

Several characteristics of play are particularly useful as diagnostic aids. The first is the child's ability to initiate play activities. Is the child a "quick starter," or does he require help in starting his play activities? Does he need encouragement and approval? Can the psychiatrist turn away momentarily from the child without disrupting the play? Is the child able to direct his play, or does he require active and steady suggestion?

The second characteristic points to the child's integration. Is the play goal-directed, or is it fragmentary? Does the play have form, or is it haphazard? Is there a short attention span with impulsive bursts of play activity, or, on the other hand, smooth and continuous play? Are there bizarre and idiosyncratic elements to the play?

The third characteristic of play pertains to the sex appropriateness of the play activity. Is the play characteristic of what is culturally expected of the sex of the child? Erikson has emphasized the gender configuration aspects of play. In a discussion of play construction scenes which he employed in child interviews, Erikson stated that he found "an analogy between the sex differences in play configuration and the primary physiological sex differences." [54] In the male the emphasis is on the external, the erectable, the intrusive, and the mobile—in the female, on the internal, on the vestibular, on the static, on what is contained and endangered in an interior. Erikson commented further that he had become accustomed to certain play configuration, segregated by sex, to the extent of taking notice when boys and girls used their counterpart's mode. Boys tend to build, maneuver, and investigate physical and mechanical properties of play objects. Girls tend to arrange by sorting and grouping, and take more care in the preservation of play material. The gender appropriateness of play in a diagnostic interview becomes more a matter of how the play is executed than whether girls play with dolls and boys play with guns. If the child's play is obviously discordant for gender, the psychiatrist observes whether there is accompanying excitement or shame. He also observes whether the play involves testing behavior and whether it becomes provocative.

The fourth characteristic tells us something about the child's creativity. Is the play imaginative or stereotyped? Is the child resourceful in the use of simple objects or does he call for special toys? Is the play mutable and amenable to improvisation or must it stay within boundaries?

The fifth characteristic indicates the child's level of maturity. Is the choice, form, or content of play infantile, age-appropriate, or precocious? Is there evidence of sudden change in the quality of play which correlates with other evidence of regression during the interview? The child will sometimes provide a self-evaluative commentary on his play.

Finally, the psychiatrist observes play for the mode and intensity of aggression. Does the child throw, tear, or destroy toys? Is there an obvious goal or purpose to the aggression or is there random assault? Does the child appear angry or impatient with his play productions? Is there evidence of clenched teeth, biting, spitting, muscular rigidity, kicking, and other belligerent poses during the play? Is most of the aggression projected, denied, or displaced through play? Does the psychiatrist anticipate danger to himself or damage to the playroom because of the fury of the child's play? If so, the psychiatrist should not stand idly by as the child evidences increasing motor aggression. He must provide controls for the child—only as required, but firmly and coupled with implied reassurance.

The six features of play can all be observed within a

relatively brief sample of play. They provide many clues to the structure and dynamics of the child's personality.

Clinical Example:

A 7-year-old girl, who had given a lengthy verbal account of herself while seated at a child's table, appeared uninterested in investigating her surroundings. She was content to draw pictures of houses with baby carriages, bicycles, and roller skates. When asked about play, she replied with some indignation that there were no suitable toys for her. She did not move from the play table for the first twenty minutes of the interview. "How did she know that the toys were not suitable?" asked the psychiatrist. She had looked at the shelf when she had first entered, she replied. The psychiatrist asked what kind of games would she like: "Oh, Cowboys and Indians and Soldiers," she responded. "Well, let's see what we have," remarked the examiner, then motioning to the toy shelf.

On the shelf were lumps of clay, various-sized clay balls, paper, a wooden mallet, paste, paper clips, a child's scissors, some string, wooden blocks, a pair of magnets, and Playdough. Looking over the contents of the shelf, the little girl said there was nothing there to play with. If the examiner did not provide guns for her, she could not play Cowboys. She was told that she could make whatever she liked. Approaching the shelf again, she noticed a lump of clay that had previously been roughly modeled in the shape of a four-legged animal. "Who did that?" she wanted to know. "Who do you think?" "You have to tell me," she said. She then disarticulated the legs from the clay body. "How many children come here?" she wanted to know. She thought that there must be many, and that they were all boys because there were no dolls. She wondered what kind of games they played. Her big brother—she was the only girl of four children—had a real gun, she remarked. Meanwhile, she was reshaping the clay. Suddenly she returned to the chair at the table. She asked: "Would you like to see what I have? My mother doesn't like me to keep it." She opened her pocketbook and exhibited an empty cartridge shell. Then she returned to the clay and said she could make a real gun, just like her brother's. She mentioned that her father had recently been hunting with her brother, and that they had shot a deer.

After she had made a clay pistol, she put the cartridge in the muzzle. Then she tried to place the gun in her small pocketbook. It would not fit. "Can I make a bag?" she asked. She was again told that she could make anything she wanted. She spent some time carefully constructing a bag from paper and paper clips. Since the end of the interview was near, she was told that shortly she would have to leave. "Can I take the gun in the bag?" "What use would you have for it?" she was asked. "Just to have and to show it to my mother." She was told that toys usually stayed in the playroom. At first, she could not accept this and tried to leave with her prize. Then suddenly she turned and moved the toy shelf away from the wall. She hid the gun in the bag behind the shelf. "You won't let anyone else play with it, will you?" she asked.

In this clinical illustration, as in many child diagnostic interviews, the characteristics of play—how the child plays—confirm the content of play. This little girl did not want substitutes for "the real thing." She was however, determined and resourceful once she had begun. She was also able to relate more warmly through play, while at the same time telling about and playing out her need to be accepted as the equal of boys. The play content underscored her concerns (offering more genetic hypotheses), whereas the characteristics of play (offering more dynamic hypotheses) illustrated her prevailing coping mechanisms.

5.

The neurological play examination: an extension of the mental status examination for children

With the expansion of community mental health centers, an increasing number of children is referred for diagnostic study. The child psychiatrist encounters a wider range of psychopathology; he has to be more alert to mental retardation and brain damage as well as to psychosocial syndromes that mimic retardation and autism but are causally related to multiple deprivation states.[30] Many more children are now evaluated who present mixed symptomatic pictures of minimal brain damage and social pathology. A common example of these diagnostic problems is that of a child who displays autistic behavior and has on examination signs of minimal to moderate CNS impairment. Phenomenologically, these children cut across many nosological categories. Whether they are *formes frustes* of clinically established syndromes or combinations of nosological entities is unclear. Nevertheless, they challenge the adequacy of child psychiatric nosology and nomenclature. These children also remind us that training and experience in child neurology are essential for child psychiatrists called upon to do diagnostic and consultative work.

Undoubtedly, the greatest deficiency in any mental status examination of children is neurological. There are many reasons for this. In his training the child psychiatrist is exposed to child neurology, but frequently the child psychiatry resident concludes that the two specialties have little in common except an interest in children. Unfortunately, the child psychiatry trainee often gains little clinical confidence from his experience in child neurology. When he encounters suspected neurological findings in a child, he is uncertain of his clinical opinion and is reluctant to refer the child to a neurologist.

If he does make the referral, he may not be able in some communities to obtain the opinion of a child neurologist who is sensitive to the presence of "soft" neurological signs in children. The general neurologist, if he has had minimal experience with children, will search mostly for "hard" signs found in blatant neurological disorders—monoparesis, cranial nerve palsy, hemianesthesia, and the like.

The most important reason for the lack of a neurological approach in the mental status examination is the objections which have been raised against a formalized neurological examination by the child psychiatrist. It has been repeatedly argued that a child is put on guard by a medical examination, which is seen by the child as authoritarian and directive.[2, 82, 106] McDonald has expressed this view: "The psychiatrist should not be the one to do the physical examination of the child. If he does the examination, he confuses the child's understanding of the psychiatrist's function and complicates the nature of the relationship the child develops with him. As stressed repeatedly . . . the psychiatrist's function is a verbal, not an active one." [109] Other clinicians have made a plea for postponement of the neurological examination until the completion of the psychodiagnostic process, with the stipulation that the examination be done by a second child psychiatrist. Still other objections are that the neurological examination, even if carried out by another physician and circumscribed with the diagnostic process, irrevocably hampers further therapy. The question has also been raised whether the child psychiatrist is qualified to do the neurological examination.

Most of the arguments raised against an incorporation of the neurological examination into the mental status examination raise the question whether the child psychiatrist can effectively and comfortably function in a multiple capacity and still be an effective psychotherapist. Obviously, the child psychiatrist's individual capacity and flexibility are crucial to the question. Nevertheless, the private practice of child psychiatry demands resourcefulness and versatility. One cannot always rely, for instance, on the opinions of a child neurologist, a speech therapist, and nursery school teacher before undertaking a therapeutic plan for a preschool child. The child psychiatrist should be able to formulate, at least provisionally, a diagnostic formulation and a treatment plan. After he has collated diagnostic findings from other consultants—and this may take several weeks and a few telephone calls—the child psychiatrist can then modify or expand, if necessary, his diagnostic and treatment formulation. Thus the child psychiatrist must be able to recognize the presence of neurological dysfunction, formulate a tentative diagnostic opinion, and ask relevant questions in communicating with his fellow consultants.

The question whether formal neurological testing adversely affects future therapy has had, we believe, validity, especially for prelatency children. The standard neurological examination in which the child is acted upon and not allowed to participate can be frightening to the child and can jeopardize the psychiatrist's relationship with the child.[56, 60] The child psychiatrist must make a bid for basic trust from the child. His approach to the child must be constant. If the psychiatrist relates to the child through play activities and verbal interchange, he should keep to this *modus operandi* in doing a neurological examination. How can a neurological examination best be done without violating these principles?

A neurological examination conducted almost entirely within the context of play is a compromise that sacrifices neither the efficacy of the neurological examination nor the psychiatrist's role as therapist. Routine neurological testing can be encompassed within the framework of play and games. Many child neurologists are themselves aware of this possibility and in certain instances and situations use play as a facilitator of testing. No attempt, however, has been made to formulate a general play approach to the child neurological examination.

The child mental status examination, we believe, is sufficiently comprehensive to alert the child psychiatrist to developmental and neurological abnormalities and deviations. How does the child psychiatrist then proceed with the neurological play examination? How does he convert the traditional neurological examination into play?

The neurological play examination is divided into six parts: (1) tests of cerebral function; (2) tests of reflexes; (3) tests of cerebellar function; (4) tests of motor system; (5) tests of the sensory system; and (6) cranial nerve testing.

1. TESTS OF CEREBRAL FUNCTION

The child mental status provides a great deal of information about cerebral functioning. For instance, perception, cognition, general intelligence, and speech supply information about cerebral functions. In the neurological examination, however, special emphasis is put on testing for apraxia, agnosia, and aphasia.

Nominal dysphasia can be tested for by a "name game" in which the child is challenged to name objects pointed out serially by the psychiatrist. "I Spy" is another game that can serve this testing purpose. Receptive dysphasia is tested immediately, following tests of nominal dysphasia, by playing "Hide and Seek" with a few of the objects. The psychiatrist asks the child to turn away while hiding some of the objects which the child has previously named. The child is then asked to find these objects sequentially—perhaps a pen, a ball, a block, and so forth.

Testing for dyspraxis is relatively easy within the context of play. Writing about apraxia in "clumsy" children, Gubbay et al.[76] described testing for apraxias of ideational, ideomotor, and motor type by "asking the child to perform complicated tasks (for example, folding a sheet of notepaper and placing it in an envelope), asking for a series of organized movements such as waving goodbye, making a fist, etc., and to demonstrate the use of objects such as a comb, toothbrush, and a spoon." They also tested children for constructional apraxia (copying designs) and dressing apraxia.

The game of "Simon Says" is particularly effective in identifying children who have aphasic and apraxic handicaps. The game starts out in "slow motion," because it is important for the child not to fail immediately. As in other parts of the neurological play examination, the simple expedient of repeating a game in which the child is denied a sensory modality (closing eyes, holding ears) can bring out defects of borderline performance. Asking a child to fold paper, place it in an envelope, seal the envelope, and tell how to mail it ("Let's play secretary") help to identify apraxic—aphasic disturbances in children.

Tests for agnosias can also be done together even though agnosia rarely affects more than one sensory mechanism. Paine has found stereognosis to be commonly defective in cerebral palsied children. Agnosias of the special senses are difficult to test for in children. Visual and auditory agnosias, however, are usually apparent during the mental status examination. Olfactory and gustatory agnosias are tested by asking the child to identify common odors and tastes. The psychiatrist is particularly attuned to noting which of the special senses the child preferentially uses.[162]

Stereognosis, graphesthesia, and texture discrimination are tested together in the game of "Blindman's Buff." Here the blindfolded child is asked to identify objects by touch. As an alternative method, the child is told to close his eyes and pretend that he is blindfolded. Common objects such as key, ball, matchbook, and paper clips are suitable for stereognostic testing. Texture discrimination is tested with a swatch of wool and satin. For graphesthesia, younger children are asked to differentiate between a traced circle and a square, and between parallel lines and a cross. Older children are tested with numbers and letters traced in their palms. In testing for graphesthesia, the test is done first with eyes open, then with eyes averted, and finally with eyes closed. Palms are tested alternately. Failure in one palm may not be conclusive unless it deviates significantly from the contralateral palm and is readily reproducible on further testing.

Testing the child's ability to estimate differences in

weight requires knowledge of the maturation of this perceptual function. Children under the age of 5 years give variable answers. Older children, however, are able to compare the weight of similar-appearing objects.

Finger agnosia is tested in a modified "This Little Piggy" game. With eyes open, the child's fingers are manipulated in different positions. Their position is reported by the child to the examiner. When the child's eyes are closed in the same game, position sense is tested. In doing these tests, the examiner must be certain that the child understands the directions. In addition, he must be certain before recording failure on these tests that the child is not intellectually impaired.

2. TESTS OF REFLEXES

Tests of reflexes include the deep tendon reflexes, pupillary reflex, and Hoffman sign. The Babinski sign is tested along with the superficial abdominal and cremasteric response during tests of sensation. The child is told that there are specific things that happen to everyone's body if a "certain command" or "special order" is given. Demonstrating on himself the knee-jerk reflex, the psychiatrist begins the "game" of reflex testing. If the child is well into latency or precociously sophisticated, the "game" becomes one of simply "taking turns." In either case, the psychiatrist demonstrates the testing method first on himself. Then he permits the child to test him, and finally he tests the child. For the occasional child who regards the reflex hammer as a real threat, preliminary use of a less frightening instrument—for instance, the tuning fork—can engage the child's interest and desensitize him to testing with a reflex hammer.

The pupillary reflex is relatively easy to test. Children are curious about penlights. If a child objects to testing of the pupillary reflex, allowing him to test the examiner's reflex will enlist the child's cooperation.

3. TESTS OF CEREBELLAR FUNCTION

Tests of cerebellar function may be left to the end, since these tests lend themselves so well to play. If the child has been restless or fidgeting, cerebellar function can be tested last. The most applicable game for testing cerebellar function is "Follow the Leader." The child follows the examiner in tandem gait, circling chairs, skipping, standing alternately on one leg and then the other. The psychiatrist notes whether there is excessive auxiliary motion brought into play; for example, "strap-hanging" or contralateral "spilling over." The Romberg sign is assessed in a game of "Playing Possum." The child is asked to remain as still as possible, with arms first at his sides, then outstretched. The game is changed into taking "pictures," with the child in various poses with his eyes open and then closed.

Diadochokinesis is tested by the familiar game of "Patty-Cake." The movements are started slowly and then accelerated. Dysmetria and past-pointing are tested in a modified game of "Pin the Tail on the Donkey." The child is told to keep his eyes open. The "donkey" is a card which the examiner moves. He urges the child to mark it with a crayon within a certain radius. The overlap of muscular coordination, cerebellar and vestibular function can be tested in another game. The child is rotated on his long axis and then asked to drop a clothespin into a wastebasket.

4. TEST OF MOTOR FUNCTION

Tests of the motor system involve examination of the form and function of skeletal musculature. If there was suggestive evidence of motor dysfunction during the mental status examination, further testing is indicated. The first game involves imitative gymnastics. The child is asked whether he can balance on one foot, do deep knee bends, push-ups, and so forth.

Some modification for gender is helpful. Boys are asked to "make a muscle" and to perform "feats of strength." Girls are usually willing to do some gymnastic exercises. The exercises are made more attractive to girls if put into dance movements.

Lower motor neuron lesions can be observed in early stages. Fasciculation and vermiform movements are elicited by reflex hammer taps on muscle. The examiner tells the child he wants to see if the hammer makes his muscles jump. He then observes the child's muscle strength. He looks for evidence of muscle wasting. The examiner should search for muscle asymmetry. The handedness and footedness of the child are taken into account in evaluating asymmetry.

Difficulty in going up or down stairs, a waddling gait, muscle weakness, hypertrophy of calf muscles, and atrophy should alert the examiner to the possibility of muscular dystrophy. In rising from a recumbent position, a child with the pseudohypertrophic type "climbs up upon himself." This characteristic sign is tested for in the game "Ring around a rosy; we all fall down."

Muscle hypertonicity is important in the evaluation of upper motor neuron lesions. If the child looks spastic, the examiner should attempt sufficiently to distract his attention in order to test whether the spasticity is emotionally influenced. "Make your arm like jelly," the child is told, while the examiner shakes the child's hand. The child may also be distracted when testing the range of motion of limbs or trunk.

Involuntary muscle movements, associated with the extrapyramidal syndromes, require careful observation. Speed of movement should be noted. Swift jerking movements—for example, myoclonic twitchings—are often confined to one muscle group. Rapid tic-like movements tend to spread from one muscle group to another. The slow, irregular, worm-like movements of athetosis may be accompanied by spasm. Choreiform movements are jerky, restless, with less spasticity of the widespread muscle groups involved. In describing tics, timing, spread, and relationship to stress are noted. Tics should be observed as fragments of larger movements which frequently have psychodynamic meaning. To test dystonic movements, twisting and torsion of the trunk and neck, the examiner should distract the child's attention by giving him a physical task to perform. Does torticollis or truncal spasm continue unaltered during push-ups or handstands? In evaluting dystonia, the child psychiatrist must be careful to avoid the organic-functional dichotomy, for often there is overlap, perhaps more so than in other involuntary movement disorders.

5. TESTS OF THE SENSORY SYSTEM

The fifth part of the neurological examination in play commences with testing of tactile sensations. The child is told to say "Boo" every time he feels something touch him. His eyes are closed during testing. This becomes a game of "gremlins," who, the child is told, will try to touch him very gently. The examiner adds that the "gremlins" must depart just as soon as the child discovers them. The examiner first uses a wisp of cotton and then a pin. Then the psychiatrist takes a tuning fork to test vibratory sense, explaining to the child that the "gremlins," having been discovered so readily, were forced to change their tactics. The tuning fork is later used for testing hearing (bone and air conduction). The same game of "gremlins" can be applied to testing position sense ("Which way is the gremlin moving your finger?") and temperature recognition ("Is this a hot or cold gremlin?").

The abdominal reflexes are most easily tested at this point in the examination. Again one can use the device of the "gremlins," who are wondering whether the child can "keep a straight face" while his abdomen is tickled. The Babinski reflex is similarly tested. The child is told to show the gremlin how still he can keep his feet. Point localization is tested by another game. The child is told that a mosquito will bite him. With his eyes closed, the child will try to catch the mosquito by placing his finger exactly at the point of the bite. At first preschool children are apt to slap at the point of stimulation, but they quickly learn to use only one finger. With older children, the game can be played with two mosquitoes that bite simultaneously. In this manner the extinction phenomenon can be tested as well as two-point discrimination.[15]

6. CRANIAL NERVE TESTING

The cranial nerves are next tested. Smell is tested optionally with vials of kitchen or household chemicals, including vinegar, mint, banana oil, and extract of onion. The child is asked to guess what the substance smells like, and to describe whether the smell is pleasant or unpleasant.

Visual acuity is tested grossly by asking the child how many fingers the examiner holds up or which way the arrow points on a rotated card. If the child is difficult to test, use of a prism or mirror facilitates the visual examination.

The third, fourth, and sixth cranial nerves are tested together with tests of ocular motility. Noting the child's eye positioning at rest, the examiner holds a penlight at a distance. He says to the child: "I bet you can't keep your eyes on this all the way." Enlisting the child's cooperation in testing convergence, he asks the child to follow the light without moving his head. The examiner can encourage the child by appearing surprised at each success. Next he uses the penlight for testing visual fields. He switches the light on and off, repeatedly marveling at the child's ability to follow the light. In all of the above testing with the penlight, except that of convergence, the child is provided with an eye cover. Although a funduscopic examination is essential for thorough testing, its incorporation into the play neurological examination is not routine. If the child is curious, funduscopy can be woven into the play atmosphere. If it is included, the pupils should be allowed to dilate in a darkened room.

The fifth cranial nerve is tested for sensory function in the general evaluation of body sensation. Its motor component is grossly assessed by having the child chew a piece of gum, slowly on one side of his mouth and then on the other. The seventh cranial nerve test becomes a game of "Making Faces." Facial asymmetry is looked for. The eleventh cranial nerve is tested along with the face-making game and includes shoulder hunching and neck movements in pantomime. The eighth cranial nerve (auditor function) is evaluated by asking a child when he can hear an approaching wrist watch. The vestibular apparatus (Cr. N. VIII) is tested by having the child whirl by using a swivel chair or making a pirouette. The remainder of the cranial nerves are examined together by playing "dentist." The child is asked to open his mouth, say "ah," swallow, protrude his tongue and wave it about.

THE HISTORY AND SIGNIFICANCE OF MINIMAL NEUROLOGICAL SIGNS

The organismic concepts of Jackson, Head, and Goldstein, derived from research on brain-injured adults, provided a great deal of clinical information which eventually was found useful in child development and psychiatry.[71, 72] Kasanin investigated personality changes in children following cerebral trauma.[92] Important work was done by Werner and Strauss in the 1940's when they studied behavioral changes in brain-damaged children.[148, 149, 165] Their findings supported Schilder's concept of minimal neurological signs, which, according to L. Bender,* came to be known as "soft" signs.[14] Strauss and Lehtinen,[147] L. Bender,[12, 13] Goldfarb,[70] Kennard,[94] Clements and Peters,[34] and others further contributed to our understanding of minimal neurological signs.[5, 6, 7, 20, 25, 36, 48, 81, 100, 118, 120, 122, 123, 125, 152, 157]

* "The concept of 'soft' neurological sign was not originally mine, but was Dr. Paul Schilder's. However, I am not aware that at any point he ever published anything which used the term . . ."[14]

The meaning of minimal neurological signs, however, is not clear. For some child neurologists and psychiatrists it means a "soft" sign or an "equivocal" sign. By contrast, a "hard" or "unequivocal" sign of neurological impairment in children is readily apparent to the clinician and incontrovertibly viewed as pathological. Hemiparesis, asymmetric deep tendon reflexes, ataxia, and marked tremor are examples of "hard" signs, the majority of which are motor in function. One "hard" sign is diagnostically worth several "soft" signs for establishing neurological deficit. "Hard" signs are less difficult to identify and interpret since they are not due to delayed maturation and are well known to most clinicians.

Another meaning of "soft" signs is that of CNS lesions which are not only structural but also pathophysiological and frequently expressed clinically as conceptual and perceptual disturbances. The disturbance can be caused by a developmental lag of the CNS—an immaturity analogous, in some ways, to the immaturity of the neonatal liver with physiological jaundice. "Soft" signs can also mean "those deviations in patterned neurological behavior which are observed in children who have developmental lags or disorders in development." [14]

No one is certain what the exact meaning of the term "soft" sign is. "The term probably means different things to different people, since it has never been clearly defined in the literature." [14] The literature on neurological signs suggestive of minimal brain damage in children demonstrates the lack of agreement in connection with what specifically are "soft" signs. Table 2 lists some "soft" signs considered by various clinicians as indicative of minimal brain damage. It is a composite of neurological signs which are indicative, either in combination or singly, of CNS structural or pathophysiological lesions. The list is not all-inclusive of "soft" neurological signs.

Table 2: NEUROLOGICAL SIGNS SUGGESTIVE OF MINIMAL BRAIN DAMAGE IN CHILDREN

Neurological Signs	Strauss & Lehtinen[147]	Goldfarb[70]	Kennard[94]	Clements & Peters[34]
Awkwardness		X	X	X
Short attention span			X	X
Hyperactivity		X	X	X
Speech defect		X	X	X
Mixed laterality			X	X
Confused laterality			X	X
Strabismus			X	X
Dysdiadochokinesia	X			
Nystagmus	X			
Tremors-choreiform movements		X		
Motor overflow		X		
Pupillary light reflex sluggish or absent	X			
Fragmentation of motor response		X		
Disturbance in posture and balance		X		
Meyer's or Leri's sign unilaterally absent	X			
Oppenheim sign	X			
Babinski sign modified				
Deficiencies in perception and conceptualization		X		
Dyslexia				X

Strauss and Lethinen regarded either a "pure" Babinski sign (dorsal extensions of the great toe with plantar flexion of the other toes) and paralysis of one of the cranial nerves (III, IV, VI, VII, or XII) as solitary neurological signs.[147] They described other neurological findings (Table 2) which singly are not significant but become meaningful if found in clusters of two or more. They placed emphasis on "the genetic period of the CNS or the time when the damage occurs [in determining] the meaning of the neurological signs at the time when the examination is made."

Kennard defined "equivocal" neurological signs as those findings which suggest CNS damage but "are so slight as to be uncertain or only occasionally and not consistently present." [94] She adds that "soft" signs often describe findings associated with more complex motor behavior. In her study of "equivocal" signs, she found visual defects, dysfunctions of extraocular motility, tremors of extended fingers, and mixed or confused laterality to be most common. She discovered, however, that controls demonstrated occasionally some of these signs. For this reason, she concluded that a true sign of organic disability must be "consistent in a single patient and of a similar pattern among groups of patients."

In a monograph on childhood schizophrenia, Goldfarb described how structural damage could be "inferred from unusual occurrences in a child's developmental history or from behavior-motor, postural, sensory-perceptual and conceptual findings." [70] Using specific neurological tests, Goldfarb was able to differentiate between what he had labeled as organic and nonorganic schizophrenic children.

With further advances in development neurology, both child psychiatrists and child neurologists will be able to make prognostic statements about the significance of "equivocal" signs. The problem of attempting a dynamic appraisal within a static examination will ease greatly as the sources of collateral information are maximized. Perspective longitudinal studies will also bring into focus the meaning of transient phenomena.

The child whose performance score falls far below his verbal score on psychometrics, whose Bender-Gestalt test is disordered, or who has lowered frustration tolerance, hyperkinesis, language disturbances, or clumsy movements will usually have what are regarded as "soft" signs on neurological testing. It is possible for a child, who at 18 months had multiple "hard" signs, in latency years to have only "soft"signs. With rapid growth of the CNS until the beginning of school years and the acquisition of new skills and compensatory mechanisms, "hard" signs often become "soft." The residue of a gross neurological defect during early development later may be found in a "soft" sign, or may not be present at all. Likewise, "soft" signs, detectable in preschool years, are often not apparent in adolescence. Their natural history, however, is not known in general, so prognostic implications of "soft" signs are not possible. Longitudinal neurological studies are needed in this clinical area.[31, 86, 89]

Knowledge of developmental neurology is essential in the recognition and evaluation of "soft" neurological signs. Peiper's text is a ready reference in developmental neurology.[122] The identification of "soft" signs requires both knowledge and experience. Thus the neurological play examination should become a familiar routine for the psychiatrist.

Attempting to learn the longitudinal developmental pattern of a child is not easy. Milestones are readily forgotten by parents. At best, milestones are unreliable data.[163] For these reasons, photographic albums and home movies are valuable sources of longitudinal developmental data. Often they are surprising documents of early neurological dysfunction. These sources are usually carefully dated and chronologically arranged by parents. Furthermore, photographic data can stimulate the parents to elaborate or emend their developmental histories. Their comments on the photographs and films provide annotations. Older children can view them and add their own commentaries.

In summary then, the neurological play examination is an adjunct to the mental status examination for those children who present subtle manifestations of CNS dysfunction. The neurological play examination can be largely encompassed within play and need not jeopardize future treatment. It is our hope that it will be improved and refined as it becomes incorporated into child psychiatric evaluations.

Appendix A

Outline of a child mental status examination

1. *Size and General Appearance*
   General health and nutrition
   Distinguishing physical characteristics or deformities
   Habit patterns
   Dress and grooming
   Apparent age versus chronological age
   Gender attributes
   General appeal
   Mannerisms and gestures
2. *Motility*
   Hyperkinesis
   Hypokinesis
   Tics and other involuntary movements
   Autoerotic movements
3. *Coordination*
   Posture and gait
   Balance
   Gross motor movements
   Fine motor movements
   Writing and drawing
4. *Speech*
   Receptive-expressive disorders
   Auditory acuity and discrimination
   Articulating defects
   Disorders of intonation

Grammar
Infantilisms of speech
Pitch and modulation
Dysrhythmias
Pronomial reversal and gender confusion
Mutism—Logorrhea
Neologisms and mannerisms of speech
5. *Intellectual Function*
General information
Vocabulary
Ability to communicate
Ability to understand and respond to questions
Learning and adapting ability
Creative talent
Social awareness
Self-help functions
6. *Modes of Thinking and Perception*
Ego-defensive mechanisms
Hallucinations
Orientation
Self-concept and body image
Identification
Peculiar verbalizations
Preoccupations and concerns
Human references
Suspiciousness and paranoid ideation
7. *Emotional Reactions*
Primary
  Fearfulness
  Sadness
  Anger
  Anxiety
  Shame
Secondary
  Apathy
  Oppositional behavior

Docility
Sulking
Appropriateness
Range of affects
Regressive pull and recovery potential
8. *Manner of Relating*
Capacity for separation and independent behavior
Friendliness
Approach-avoidance
Aggressivity
Need for approval
Age level (regressed or precocious)
Adaptability
9. *Fantasies and Dreams*
Dreams
Symbolic elaboration versus undisguised concrete
representation
Fantasies
Stories
Wishes
Ambitions
10. *Character of Play*
Formal characteristics
Gender configurations
Transactional aspects
Characteristics versus contents

Appendix B

Some common questions used in a child mental status examination

Questions are listed in a rough temporal sequence for the interview. They are best asked during activity and not during static face-to-face confrontation. If the child does not answer a question, it should be rephrased rather than exactly repeated. Bridging phrases are helpful: for example, "I wonder if . . ." and "Do you suppose . . ." and "How about telling me . . ."

Name:
  What do people call you?
  Do you have a nickname?
Age:
  How old are you?
  When is your next birthday?
Home:
  Who lives at home?
  What is your father's work?
  Does your mother work?
  What does your house look like?
  Do you have your own bedroom? Your own bed?
  Suppose you were showing me around your house, what would you like to show me?
  Do you and your parents spend a lot of time in the kitchen?
School:
  What grade are you in at school?

Who helps you with your homework?

What kinds of things do you do in school?

What part of school do you like best?

Attitudes and Ideas about Interview:

What would you call this place?

Do you know why children come here?

Did your mother tell you something about coming here today?

What kind of things did you think we would talk about?

Ambitions—Identifications:

What would you like to do when you grow up?

Have you ever thought of some other thing?

Do you take after your mother or father?

Who is your hero—heroine?

Self-Image:

If you could change something about yourself, what would that be?

Do you get angry with yourself sometimes? About what?

(Age 4–8) Do you dress yourself? Can you tie your shoelaces? Can you tell time?

Are you a good runner?

Are most of the boys/girls your age bigger or smaller than you?

Socialization:

Who is your best friend?

What kinds of things do you do together?

Can you get into games easily?

Have you ever stayed with your friend overnight?

Have you ever gone to day or sleepover camp?

Has your friend ever stayed at your house overnight? How did you feel eating and sleeping at her/his house?

How do you and your brothers/sisters get along?

Hobbies and Games:

Do you save things?

What is your favorite toy? Game? Interest after school?

What kinds of things can you make? Who helps you?
What game do you play best? Whom do you play with?
Wishes:
  If you had three magic wishes, what would they be?
  What would you do with a lot of money?
  What things would you buy?
  What is the best age to be?
Dreams, Fantasies, and Early Memories:
  What is something you can remember that happened a
    long time ago?
  Tell me a dream you have had. How about a daydream?
  Do dreams ever scare you?
Return to the Chief Complaint:
  What do you think could worry your parents about you?
  What kind of worries might you have?
  Your mother tells me that she worries about _____;
    What can you tell me about that?
  What could make you unhappy or sad?
  What kind of things might you have been scolded for
    lately?
Fears:
  What kinds of things are you afraid of?
  Were you afraid of coming here?
  Maybe you have some question for me.
  Was this (interview) like what you thought it would be?
  Do you like to get up in the morning?
  How about going to sleep at night?

Appendix C

Outline of the neurological play examination: useful play and games

1. *Cerebral Functions*
   "Naming game," "I Spy"
   "Hide and Seek"
   "Let's make things"
   "Let's copy these designs"
   "Simon Says"
   "Blindman's Buff"
   "This Little Piggy . . ."
2. *Reflexes*
   "Let's give a command to the body"
   "Let's take turns"
3. *Cerebellar Function*
   "Follow the Leader"
   "Playing Possum"
   "Picture Taking"
   "Patty-Cake"
   "Pin the Tail on the Donkey"
   "Drop the Clothespin"
4. *Motor Functions*
   Imitative gymnastics
   "Make a fist"
   Indian wrestling
   "Let's see you dance"
   "Let's see the muscle jump"
   "Make your arm like jelly"

"Ring around a rosy; we all fall down"
5. *Sensory Functions*
   "Say 'Boo' to the gremlin"
   "Which way is the gremlin moving your toe?"
   "Hot or cold gremlin?"
   "Point to the mosquito bite"
   "How many mosquito bites—one or two?"
6. *Cranial Nerves*
   "Have you ever smelled this?"
   "Follow the penlight; I bet you can't keep your eyes on this all the way around."
   "Chew a piece of gum on each side of your mouth."
   "Let's see you make monkey faces"
   Neck and face movements in pantomime
   "Let's play dentist: Open mouth, say 'ah,' swallow, protrude tongue and move tongue."

References

1. ACKERMAN, N. W.: *The Psychodynamics of Family Life.* New York: Basic Books, 1958.
2. ALLEN, F. H.: *Psychotherapy with Children.* New York: Norton, 1942.
3. ANTHONY, E. J., AND SCOTT, P.: Manic-Depressive Psychosis in Childhood, *J. Child Psychol. Psychiat.,* 1:53–72, 1959.
4. APPEL, K. E., AND STRECHER, E. A.: *Practical Examination of Personality and Behavior Disorders.* New York: Macmillan Co., 1936.
5. BAKWIN, H.: Cerebral Damage and Behavior Disorders in Children, *J. Pediat.,* 34:371–382, 1949.
6. BAKWIN, H. (ED.): *Symposium on Behavior Disorders,* Ped. Clinics N. America. Philadelphia: W. B. Saunders Co., August, 1958.
7. BAX, M., AND MAC KEITH, R. (EDS.): *Minimal Cerebral Dysfunction.* London: Heinemann, 1963.
8. BEISER, H. R.: Play Equipment for Diagnosis and Therapy, *Am. J. Orthopsychiat.,* 25:761–770, 1955.
9. BEISER, H. R.: Psychiatric Diagnostic Interviews with Children, *J. Am. Acad. Child Psychiat.,* 1:656–670, 1962.
10. BELLER, E. K.: *Clinical Process.* Glencoe, Ill.: The Free Press, 1962.
11. BENDER, L.: *Child Psychiatric Technique.* Springfield, Ill.: Charles C Thomas, 1952.
12. BENDER, L.: *A Dynamic Psychopathology of Childhood.* Springfield, Ill.: Charles C Thomas, 1954.
13. BENDER, L.: *Psychopathology of Children with Organic*

Brain Disorders. Springfield, Ill.: Charles C Thomas, 1956.

14. BENDER, L.: Personal communication, 1965.

15. BENDER, M. B.: *Disorders in Perception.* Springfield, Ill.: Charles C Thomas, 1952.

16. BENJAMIN, J. D.: Developmental Biology and Psychoanalysis, In N. S. Greenfield and W. L. Lewis (eds.): *Psychoanalysis and Current Biological Thought.* Madison and Milwaukee: University of Wisconsin Press, 1965, pp. 57–80.

17. BERG, C.: *The First Interview with a Psychiatrist.* Liverpool: George Allen, 1956.

18. BERLIN, I. N.: *Bibliography of Child Psychiatry.* Washington, D.C.: American Psychiatric Association, 1963.

19. BINET, A., AND SIMON, T.: Upon the Necessity of Establishing a Scientific Diagnosis of Inferior Status of Intelligence, In W. Dennis (ed.), *Readings in the History of Psychology.* New York: Appleton-Century-Crofts, 1948, pp. 407–411.

20. BIRCH, H. G. (ED.): *Brain Damage in Children.* Philadelphia: The Williams & Wilkins Co., 1964.

21. BIRD, B.: *Talking with Patients.* Philadelphia: Lippincott, 1955.

22. BIRDWHISTELL, R. L.: The Tertiary Sexual Characteristics of Man: A Fundamental in Human Communication, A.A.A.S. Meeting, Montreal, 1964.

23. BOTT, H. M.: Observations of Play Activities in a Nursery School, *Genet. Psychol. Monograph,* 4:44–88, 1928.

24. BOWLBY, J.: The Nature of the Child's Tie to His Mother, *Int. J. Psycho-Anal.* 39:350–373, 1958.

25. BRADLEY, C.: The Behavior of Children Receiving Benzedrine, *Am. J. Psychiat.,* 94:577–585, 1937.

26. BRAIN, R. W.: *Diseases of the Nervous System.* Oxford: London University Press, 1956, p. 106.

27. BURDOCK, E. I., AND HARDESTY, A. S.: *Children's Behavior Inventory*. Biometrics Research, Columbia University and New York State Department of Mental Hygiene, 1964.

28. BURDOCK, E. D., AND HARDESTY, A. S.: Children's Behavior Diagnostic Inventory, *Annals N.Y. Acad. Science*, 105:890–896, 1964.

29. CAMERON, K.: Diagnostic Categories in Child Psychiatry, *Brit. J. Med. Psychol.*, 28:67–71, 1955.

30. CAPLAN, G. (ED.): *Emotional Problems of Early Childhood*. New York: Basic Books, 1955.

31. CAPLAN, H., BIBACE, R., AND RABINOVITCH, M. S.: Paranatal Stress, Cognitive Organization and Ego Function: A Controlled Follow-Up Study of Children Born Prematurely, *J. Am. Acad. Child Psychiat.*, 2:434–450, 1963.

32. CHESS, S.: *An Introduction to Child Psychiatry*. New York: Grune & Stratton, 1959.

33. CHESS, S., THOMAS, A., RUTTER, M., AND BIRCH, H. G.: Interaction of Temperament and Environment in the Production of Behavioral Disturbances in Children, *Am. J. Psychiat.*, 120:142–147, 1963.

34. CLEMENTS, S. D., AND PETERS, J. E.: Minimal Brain Dysfunction in the School-Age Child, *A.M.A. Arch. Gen. Psychiat.*, 6:185–197, 1962.

35. COLEMAN, J. V., SHORT, G. B., AND HIRSCHBERG, J. C.: The Intake Interview as the Beginning of Psychiatric Treatment in Children's Cases, *Am. J. Psychiat.*, 105:183–186, 1948.

36. COMLY, H. H.: Diffuse Brain Damage in Children: Behavioral Manifestations, *Lancet*, 75:187–190, 1955.

37. CONN, J. H.: The Play-Interview: A Method of Studying Children's Attitudes, *Am. J. Dis. Children*, 58:1199–1214, 1939.

38. DARWIN, C.: A Biographical Sketch of an Infant, *Mind*, 2:285–294, 1877.

39. DÉCARIE, T. G.: *Intelligence and Affectivity in Early Childhood*. New York: International Universities Press, 1965.

40. DE HIRSCH, K.: Studies in Tachyphemia: IV: Diagnosis of Developmental Language Disorders, *Logos*, 4:3–9, 1961.

41. DE HIRSCH, K., AND JANSKY, J. J.: Language Investigation of Children Suffering from Familial Dysartonomia, *J. Speech Hearing Disorders*, 2:450–460, 1956.

42. DE SAINT EXUPÉRY, A.: *The Little Prince*. New York: Harcourt, Brace, and World, 1943.

43. DESPERT, J. L.: Technical Approaches Used in the Study and Treatment of Emotional Problems in Children. Part Five: The Playroom, *Psychiat. Quart.*, 11:677–696, 1937.

44. DESPERT, J. L.: *Emotional Problems in Children*. Utica: State Hospital Press, 1938.

45. DESPERT, J. L.: Delusional and Hallucinatory Experiences in Children, *Am. J. Psychiat.*, 104:528–537, 1948.

46. DEUTSCH, F., AND MURPHY, W.: *The Clinical Interview*. New York: International Universities Press, 1955.

47. DOWNS, J. L.: On Some of the Mental Affections of Childhood and Youth, *The Lettsonian Lectures of the Medical Society of London*, 1887.

48. EISENBERG, L.: Psychiatric Implications of Brain Damage in Children, *Psychiat. Quart.*, 31:72–86, 1957.

49. EISENBERG, L.: Hallucinations in Children. In L. J. West (ed.), *Hallucinations*. New York: Grune & Stratton, 1962, pp. 198–210.

50. EISENBERG, L.: Office Examination of Specific Reading Disability in Children, *Ped.*, 23:997–1007, 1953.

51. ENGEL, M.: Some Parameters of the Psychological Evaluation of the Child, *A.M.A. Arch. Gen. Psychiat.*, 2:593–605, 1960.

52. ERICKSON, C. E.: Guidance in Secondary Schools. In E. Harins (ed.), *Handbook of Child Guidance*. New York: Child Care Publishers, 1947, p. 102.

53. ERIKSON, E. H.: *Childhood and Society*. New York: W. W. Norton, 1950, pp. 49–50.

54. ERIKSON, E. H.: Sex Differences in Play Construction of Twelve-Year-Old Children. In J. Tanner, and B. Inhelder (eds.), *Discussions on Child Development*, Vol. III. New York: International Universities Press, 1958, p. 112.

55. ESCALONA, S., AND HEIDER, G.: *Prediction and Outcome.* New York: Basic Books, 1959.

56. FARMER, T. W. (ED.): *Pediatric Neurology*. New York: Hoeber Medical Division, 1964.

57. FINCH, S. M.: *Fundamentals of Child Psychiatry*. New York: Norton, 1960.

58. FLAVELL, J. H.: *The Developmental Psychology of Jean Piaget*. New York: D. Van Nostrand Company, 1963.

59. FLETCHER, W. B.: Mental Development and Insanity of Children, *Int. Clinic*, 5:138–147, 1895.

60. FORD, F. R.: *Diseases of the Nervous System in Infancy, Childhood and Adolescence* (4th ed.). Springfield, Ill.: Charles C Thomas, 1960, pp. 1187–1188.

61. FRAIBERG, S. H.: *The Magic Years*. New York: Scribner's, 1959.

62. FREUD, A.: Assessment of Childhood Disturbances, *Psychoanal. Study Child*, 17:149–158, 1962.

63. FREUD, A.: *Normality and Pathology in Childhood*. New York: International Universities Press, 1965, p. 11.

64. FREUD, S. Inhibitions, Symptoms and Anxiety, *Standard Edition*, 20:87–174. London: Hogarth Press, 1959.

65. GALDSTON, R.: Observations of Children Who Have Been Physically Abused by Their Parents, *Am. J. Psychiat.*, 122:440–443, 1965.

66. GESELL, A. L.: *The Child from Five to Ten*. New York: Harper, 1946.

67. GESELL, A., AND ARMATRUDA, C.: *Developmental Diagnosis.* New York: P. B. Hoeber, 1947.

68. GILL, M., NEWMAN, R., AND REDLICH, F.: *The Initial Interview in Psychiatric Practice.* New York: International Universities Press, 1954.

69. GOLD, A.: Personal communication, 1966.

70. GOLDFARB, W.: *Childhood Schizophrenia.* Cambridge: Harvard University Press, 1961.

71. GOLDSTEIN, K.: *The Organism. A Holistic Approach to Biology Derived from Pathological Data in Man.* New York: American Book Co., 1939.

72. GOLDSTEIN, K.: *After-Effects of Brain-Injuries in War.* New York: Grune & Stratton, 1942.

73. GREENACRE, P.: Review of *Practical Examination of Personality and Behavior Disorders* by K. E. Appel and E. A. Stricker. *Psychoanal. Quart.,* 6:134, 1937

74. GROUP FOR THE ADVANCEMENT OF PSYCHIATRY (G.A.P.): *The Diagnostic Process in Child Psychiatry, Report No. 38.* New York: Group for the Advancement of Psychiatry, 1957.

75. GROUP FOR THE ADVANCEMENT OF PSYCHIATRY (G.A.P.): *Psychopathological Disorders in Childhood: Theoretical Considerations and a Proposed Classification, Report No. 62.* New York: Group for the Advancement of Psychiatry, 1966.

76. GUBBAY, S. S., ELLIS, E., WALTON, J. N., AND COURT, S. D. M.: Clumsy Children. A Study of Apraxic and Agnosic Defects in 21 Children, *Brain,* 88: 295–312, 1965.

77. HALL, G. S.: The Contents of Children's Minds on Entering School, *Ped. Sem.,* 1:139–173, 1891.

78. HALL, M. B.: *Psychiatric Examination of the School Child.* Baltimore: Williams & Wilkins, 1947.

79. HARRIS, E.: *Handbook of Child Guidance.* New York: Child Care Publications, 1947.

80. HARRISON, S. I., HESS, J. H., AND ZRULL, J. P.: Paranoid

Reactions in Children, *J. Am. Acad. Child Psychiat.*, 2:677–691, 1963.

81. HARWIK, L. J., NELSON, S. E., HANSON, H. B., ANDERSON, A. S., DRESSLER, W. H., AND ZARLING, V. R.: Diagnosis of Cerebral Dysfunction in Children, *Am. J. Dis. Child*, 101:364–375, 1961.

82. HAWORTH, M. R. (ED.): *Child Psychotherapy*. New York: Basic Books, 1964.

83. HOLMES, C.: Insanity in Childhood, *N.Y. Med. J.*, 95:283–294, 1912.

84. HOMBURGER, A.: *Vorlesungen über Psychopathologie des Kinderalters*. Berlin: J. Springer, 1926.

85. HUG-HELLMUTH, H. VON: *Aus dem Seelenleben des Kindes. Eine Psychoanalytische Studie*. Leipzig and Vienna: Franz Deuticke, 1913.

86. ILLINGSWORTH, R. S.: *The Development of the Infant and Young Child*. Edinburgh and London: E. &. S. Livingstone, 1960.

87. INHELDER, B.: Criteria of the Stages of Mental Development. In J. M. Tanner and B. Inhelder (eds.), *Discussions on Child Development*, Vol. 1. New York: International Universities Press, 1955.

88. INSTITUTE FOR JUVENILE RESEARCH: *Child Guidance Procedures*. New York: Appleton, 1937.

89. KAGAN, J., AND MOSS, H. A.: *Birth to Maturity*. New York: Wiley, 1962.

90. KAHN, R., AND CANNELL, C.: *The Dynamics of Interviewing*. New York: Wiley, 1963.

91. KANNER, L.: *Child Psychiatry* (1st ed.). Springfield, Ill.: Charles C Thomas, 1935.

92. KASANIN, J.: Personality Changes in Children Following Cerebral Trauma, *J. Nerv. Ment. Dis.*, 69:385–406, 1929.

93. KATAN, A.: Some Thoughts about the Role of Verbalization in Early Childhood, *Psychoanal. Study Child*, 16:184–188, 1961.

94. KENNARD, M. A.: The Value of Equivocal Signs in Neurologic Diagnosis, *Neurol.* (Minneapolis), 10:753–764, 1960.

95. KESSLER, J. W.: *Psychopathology of Childhood.* Englewood Cliffs: Prentice-Hall, 1966.

96. KRUG, O. (EXECUTIVE ED.): *Career Training in Child Psychiatry.* Washington, D.C.: American Psychiatric Association, 1964, p. 63.

97. LANGFORD, W. S.: Anxiety Attacks in Children, *Am. J. Orthopsychiat.*, 7: 210–218, 1937.

98. LANGFORD, W. S.: Reflections on Classification in Child Psychiatry as Related to the Activities of the Committee on Child Psychiatry of the Group for the Advancement of Psychiatry. In R. L. Jenkins and J. O. Cole (eds.) *Diagnostic Classification in Child Psychiatry:* Psychiatric Research Report No. 18, Washington, D.C.: American Psychiatric Association, 1964, p. 4.

99. LAURENDEAU, M., AND PINARD, A.: *Causal Thinking in the Child.* New York: International Universities Press, 1962.

100. LAWRENCE, M. M.: Minimal Brain Damage in Child Psychiatry, *Comp. Psychiat.*, 1:360–369, 1960.

101. LAYMAN, E. M., AND LOWRIE, R. S.: Waiting Room Observation as a Technique for Analysis of Communication Behavior in Children and Their Parents. In P. Hoch and J. Zubin (eds.), *Psychopathology of Communication.* New York: Grune & Stratton, 1958.

102. LEVY, D. M.: A Method for Determining the Mental Age during a Physical Examination, *A.M.A. Arch. Neurol. Psychiat.*, 11: 669–673, 1924.

103. LEVY, D. M.: The Physiologic and Psychiatric Examination, *Am. J. Psychiat.*, 9: 121–194, 1929.

104. LEVY, D. M.: Use of Play Technic as Experimental Procedure, *Am. J. Orthopsychiat.*, 3:266–277, 1933.

105. LEVY, D. M.: Release Therapy in Young Children, *Psychiat.*, 1:387–390, 1938.

106. LIPPMANN, H. S.: *Treatment of the Child in Emotional Conflict.* New York: McGraw-Hill, 1962.

107. MALMQUIST, C. P.: Problems of Confidentiality in Child Psychiatry, *Am. J. Orthopsychiat.*, 35:787–792, 1965.

108. MARTIN, F., AND KNIGHT, J.: Joint Interview as Part of Intake Procedure in a Child Psychiatric Clinic, *J. Child Psychol. Psychiat.*, 3:17–26, 1962.

109. MC DONALD, M.: The Psychiatric Evaluation of Children, *J. Am. Acad. Child Psychiat.*, 4:569–612, 1965.

110. MAIER, H. W.: *Three Theories of Child Development.* New York: Harper & Row, 1965.

111. MEYER, A.: Schedule for the Study of Mutual Abnormalities in Children. In *Handbook of Illinois Society for Child Study*, 1895, p. 53.

112. MONROE, M.: *Children Who Cannot Read.* Chicago: University of Chicago Press, 1932.

113. MURPHY, L. B., AND COLLABORATORS: *The Widening World of Childhood.* New York: Basic Books, 1962, pp. 321–341.

114. MUSSEN, P. H., CONGER, J. J., AND KAGAN, J. (EDS.): *Child Development and Personality* (2nd ed.). New York: Harper & Row, 1963.

115. MUSSEN, P. H., CONGER, J. J., AND KAGAN, J. (EDS.): *Readings in Child Development and Personality.* New York: Harper & Row, 1965.

116. NEUBAUER, P., ALPERT, A., AND BANKS, B.: The Nursery Group Experience as Part of a Diagnostic Study of a Pre-School Child. In Esman, A. (ed.), *New Frontiers of Child Guidance.* New York: International Universities Press, 1958.

117. NEUBAUER, P. B.: Panel Report: Psychoanalytic Contributions to the Nosology of Child Psychic Disorders, *J. Am. Psychoanal. Asso.*, 11:595–604, 1963.

118. NYLANDER, I., AND KOERNER, P. E.: Electroencephalography and Cerebral Lesions: A Clinical Investigation on Children, *J. Clin. Psychopath.*, 13:164–174, 1952.
119. ORTON, S. T.: *Reading, Writing and Speech Problems in Children.* New York: Norton, 1937.
120. PAINE, R. S.: Minimal Chronic Brain Syndromes in Children, *Devel. Med. Child Neurol.*, 4: 21–35, 1962.
121. PAINE, R. S.: The Contributions of Neurology to the Pathogenesis of Hyperactivity in Children, *Clin. Proc. Child. Hospital* (Washington, D.C.), 19:235–247, 1963.
122. PEIPER, A.: *Cerebral Function in Infancy and Childhood* (3rd ed.). New York: Consultants Bureau, 1963.
123. PERLSTEIN, M. A. (ED.): *Symposium on Neuropediatrics, Ped. Clinic. N. America.* Philadelphia: W. B. Saunders, August 1960.
124. PIAGET, J.: *The Child's Conception of the World.* New York: Harcourt, Brace, 1929.
125. PINCUS, J. H., AND GLASER, G. H.: The Syndrome of "Minimal Brain Damage" in Childhood, *New England J. Med.*, 275:27–35, 1966.
126. PRINCE, G. S.: A Clinical Approach to Parent-Child Interaction, *J. Child. Psychol. Psychiat.*, 2:169–184, 1961.
127. PRITCHARD, M.: Observation of Children in a Psychiatric In-Patient Unit, *Brit. J. Psychiat.*, 109:572–578, 1963.
128. RACHMAN, S., AND BERGER, M.: Whirling and Postural Control in Schizophrenic Children, *J. Child Psychol. Psychiat.*, 4:137–155, 1963.
129. REDL, F.: The Life Space Interview in the School Setting Workshops, 1961, *Am. J. Orthopsychiat.*, 33: 717–733, 1963.
130. RENFREW, C., AND MURPHY, K. (EDS.): *The Child Who Does Not Talk.* London: Heinemann, 1964.

131. REXFORD, E. N.: The Life Space Interview, Workshop, 1957, Am. J. Orthopsychiat., 29:1–44, 1959.
132. ROBINSON, J. F., VITALE, L. J., AND NITSCHE, C. J.: Behavioral Categories of Childhood, Am. J. Psychiat., 117:806–810, 1961.
133. ROGERS, C. R.: The Clinical Treatment of the Problem Child. Boston: Houghton Mifflin, 1939.
134. ROSS, A. O., LACEY, H. M., AND PARTON, D. A.: The Development of a Behavior Checklist for Boys, Child Develop., 36:1013–1027, 1965.
135. SCHILDER, P.: Contributions to Developmental Neuropsychiatry (L. Bender, ed.). New York: International Universities Press, 1964, p. x.
136. SCHLEIFER, M.: The Clinical Process and Research Methodology, J. Am. Acad. Child Psychiat., 2:72–98, 1963.
137. SCHOPLER, E.: Early Infantile Autism and Receptor Processes, A.M.A. Arch. Gen. Psychiat., 13:327–335, 1965.
138. SEARS, R. R.: Child Psychology. In W. Dennis (ed.), Current Trends in Psychology. Pittsburgh: University of Pittsburgh Press, 1947, pp. 50–74.
139. SHIRLEY, H. F.: Psychiatry for the Pediatrician. New York: Commonwealth Fund, 1948.
140. SHIRLEY, H. F.: Pediatric Psychiatry. Cambridge: Harvard University Press, 1963.
141. SILVER, A. A.: Psychologic Aspects of Pediatrics, Postural and Righting Responses in Children, J. Ped., 41:493–498, 1952.
142. SILVER, A. A.: Three Drawing Tests for Children, J. Ped., 37:129–143, 1950.
143. SIMMONS, J. E.: Personal communication, 1965.
144. SIMONS, G. S., AND GILLIES, S. M.: Some Physical Characteristics of a Group of Psychotic Children, Brit. J. Psychiat., 110:104–107, 1964.

145. SODDY, K.: *Clinical Child Psychiatry*. London: Bailliere, Tindall and Cox, 1960.
146. SPITZ, R. A.: *The First Year of Life*. New York: International Universities Press, 1965.
147. STRAUSS, A. A., AND LEHTINEN, L. E.: *Psychopathology and Education of the Brain-Injured Child*. 2 vols. New York: Grune & Stratton, 1947.
148. STRAUSS, A., AND WERNER, H.: The Mental Organization of the Brain-Injured Mentally Defective Child, *Am. J. Psychiat.*, 97: 1195–1203, 1941.
149. STRAUSS, A., AND WERNER, H.: Disorders of Conceptual Thinking in the Brain-Injured Child, *J. Nerv. Ment. Dis.*, 96:153–172, 1942.
150. SULLIVAN, H. S.: *The Collected Works of Harry Stack Sullivan*, Vol. II (H. S. Perry, M. L. Gorvel, and M. Gibbon, eds.). New York: Norton, 1956, p. 301.
151. SULLIVAN, H. S.: *The Psychiatric Interview*. New York: Norton, 1954.
152. TARDIEN, G., MONFRAIX, C., TABARY, J. C., AND TARDIEN, C.: Troubles de la Reconnaissance Mamielle des Formes chez l'enfant Atteint d'Infirmité Morice Cérébrale, *Rev. Neurol.*, 105:480–488, 1961.
153. TEICHER, J. D.: Preliminary Survey of Motility in Children, *J. Nerv. Ment. Dis.*, 94:277–304, 1941.
154. THOMÄ, H.: Beobachtung und Beurteilung von Dindern und Jugendlichen, *Psychologische Praxis*, 15:1–64, 1953.
155. THOMAS, A., CHESS, S., BIRCH, H. G., HERTZIG, M. E., AND KORN, S.: *Behavioral Individuality in Early Childhood*. New York: New York University Press, 1963.
156. TOOLAN, J. M.: Depression in Children and Adolescents, *Am. J. Orthopsychiat.*, 32:404–415, 1962.
157. TRAINER, M.: Problems of Child Neurology, *Ther. Umsch.*, 14: 36–40, 1957.
158. VAN AMERONGEN, S.: Initial Psychiatric Family Studies, *Am. J. Orthopsychiat.*, 24:73–83, 1954.

159. WAELDER, R.: The Psychoanalytic Theory of Play, *Psychoanal. Quart.*, 2:208–224, 1933.

160. WATSON, J. B., AND RAGNOR, R.: Conditioned Emotional Reactions, *J. Exp. Psychol.*, 3:1–14, 1920.

161. WATSON, R. I.: *Psychology of the Child.* New York: Wiley, 1963, pp. 3–37.

162. WEDELL, K.: The Visual Perception of Cerebral Palsied Children, *J. Child Psychol. Psychiat.*, 1:215–227, 1960.

163. WENAR, C.: The Reliability of Developmental Histories, *Psychosom. Med.*, 25:505–509, 1963.

164. WERKMAN, S. L.: The Psychiatric Diagnostic Interview with Children, *Am. J. Orthopsychiat.*, 35:764–771, 1965.

165. WERNER, H.: Comparative Psychopathology of the Brain-Injured Child and the Traumatic Brain-Injured Adult, *Am. J. Psychiat.*, 99:835–838, 1943.

166. WILE, I. S., AND DAIRS, R.: The Relation of Birth to Behavior, *Am. J. Orthopsychiat.*, 12:104–114, 1942.

167. WILKING, V. N., AND PAOLI, C.: The Hallucinatory Experience: An Attempt at a Psychodynamic Classification and Reconsideration of Its Diagnostic Significance, *J. Am. Acad. Child Psychiat.*, 5:431–440, 1966.

168. WITMER, H. L. (ED.): *Psychiatric Interviews with Children.* New York: Commonwealth Fund, 1946.

169. WOLFF, P. H.: Developmental and Motivational Concepts in Piaget's Sensorimotor Theory of Intelligence, *J. Am. Acad. Child Psychiat.*, 2:225–243, 1963.

170. YARROW, L. J.: Interviewing Children. In P. H. Mussen (ed.), *Handbook of Research Methods in Child Development.* New York: Wiley, 1960, pp. 561–602.

171. YOUNG, L.: Diagnosis as a Creative Process, *Soc. Casework*, 37:275–280, 1956.

172. ZUBIN, J.: Classification of the Behavior Disorders, *Ann. Review Psychol,* in press.

Index

perception, 23, 91; modes of, 39, 61–67, 108
perceptual-motor apparatus, neurophysiological immaturity of, 52
personality function, assessment of, 6, 7, 9, 31
perspiration, excessive, 42
Peters, J. E., 101
phobic mechanisms, 62, 65
physical appearance, 15–16, 18, 23, 39, 41–45, 107
physical contact, avoidance of, 74–75
physical examinations, 41–43, 88–89
physically handicapped children, examination of, 34
Piaget, J., 5, 62
play, character of, 80–86, 109
play therapy, 5, 6, 8–9, 11, 13, 15, 18, 30–31, 48–52, 56, 61, 68, 74–77, 80–86; see also games
point localization, testing of, 99
poise, 58, 68
position sense, testing of, 98–99
posture, 18, 43, 48–49, 107
prognosis, 22, 105
provocative behavior, 47, 63, 75, 78, 82
psychiatric nosology, 3–5, 7, 8, 87; international, need for, 19
psychiatric social workers, 5, 10, 17, 21
psychodiagnostic formulations, 21, 22
psychological tests, 13, 18–19, 22, 43
psychometrics, 59–61, 105
pupillary reflex, testing of, 95

rapport, establishment of, 8, 38
rashes, 42
reading, 18, 51, 52; reversal in, 53
reality testing, 76
reassurance, need for, 75, 81
recording equipment, 36
regression(s), 25, 46, 47, 59, 83; transient, 17, 24
regression rate, 33
relating, manner of, 72–77, 109
restlessness, 45, 48, 66, 71, 95
reticence, 47
riddles, 70
rocking, 46

role-playing, 9
Romberg test, 52, 95
Rorschach Psychodiagnostic Battery, 19

sadness, 68, 69, 72, 108
salivation, excessive, 42
scanning speech, 56
scars, 42
Schilder, Paul, 101
schizophrenia, hallucinations and, 62–63; neurological study on, 104
school behavior, information on, 14–15
school "phobics," 26
scratching, 46
seizure activity, signs of, 42
self-concept, 9, 33, 64–65, 108
sensorium, altered, 47
sensory system, testing of, 94, 98–99
separation-individualization, 26
sex characteristics, 26 n., 82
sex differences, 25–26; and motor function testing, 96; in play configuration, 82; and reaction to psychiatrist, 75
sex-role identification, 43
sexual material, 16
shame, 68, 108
Shirley, H. F., 6
shyness, 26, 69–70
sibling rivalry, 73
similarities-differences, ability in handling, 18
Simmons, J., 9
smell, testing of, 93, 99
smiling, 69
socialization, 48
Soddy, K., 6
"soft" neurological signs, 88, 101–106
somnolence, 42, 47
spasms, 97; habit, 42, 46; truncal, 98
spasticity, 97
speech, 15–16, 18, 23, 39, 52–57, 80, 107–108; age norms and, 52, 56; aphasia and, 53–57; articulation defects, 54–57, 107; blocking in, 15, 56; CNS damage and, 56; dysrhythmias of, 56, 108; evaluation of, areas